AF571888

TIME AND TIM REMEMBERED

A Tradition of Bay Area Architecture

Pflueger Architects
Timothy, Milton and John

The First Seventy-Five Years
1908 to 1983

Milton T. Pflueger

Designed and produced by Pflueger Architects
and Terry Pimsleur & Company, San Francisco, CA

Cover medallion reproduced from the Mayan motif elevator fronts
in the lobby of 450 Sutter Street, San Francisco

Published by Pflueger Architects
165 10th Street, San Francisco, CA 94103

Library of Congress Catalogue Card Number 84-90603
ISBN 0-9614133-0-1
Printed in the United States of America.

My sweetheart, with Johnnie, as we called him when he was a little fellow.

To My Sweetheart

"Earth's noblest thing, a woman perfected"

Lowell

The year 1982 marked the end of an earthly life of purest beauty. No changes were made in the text of the book. As it was at the time of writing, indeed, as in all the years of our love, neither do I now have the words for a heart filled with thanksgiving.

March 1983

CONTENTS

Timothy Pflueger's great significance as a high-rise architect lay in the emotional power of his towers, which frankly expressed industrial technology, but nevertheless achieved poetic meanings that the International Stylists, in the name of structural rationalism, were ironing out of their designs. The steel-frames of his structures are basically truthful, but architecture is more than structural veracity; and exactitude, as Matisse said, is not truth. By going beyond a functionalist esthetic to a personalized romanticism that deserves comparison not only with Saarinen's, but also with Frank Lloyd Wright's in the 1920s, Pflueger also gave himself room for outright fantasy in his theatrical work, particularly the Paramount in Oakland, one of the finest "picture palaces." This mood of controlled opulence, and clear practical purpose, later was purified in the austere white marble surfaces of I. Magnin in Union Square.

Allan Temko, Architectural Critic,
SAN FRANCISCO CHRONICLE

FOREWORD

By Harold Gilliam

This book is a warm personal portrait of a man whose architectural signature is emblazoned across the skyline of San Francisco and whose career symbolized the efforts of the city—and the era—to find its own architectural identity. It is also the story of how the vigorously innovative thrust he initiated has been continued by his brother and his nephew and is currently taking new directions into the revolutionary architectural era beginning.

Before the story opens, permit me some reminiscences of my own. I first came to the Bay Area to be a student at Berkeley, and from the University campus I often gazed across the bay at the incredible monoliths of San Francisco rising on hills above the water like the towers of some modern Camelot. On weekends we would close the books and head for that magic city on the horizon, our nerve-ends fairly crackling with excitement.

Going west on the Bay Bridge, watching the city loom larger as we approached, I had the illusion that the towers were growing there in front of me at that moment; they seemed to rise into the sky as if thrust up by some geologic force deep in the earth.

Gradually the skyline would resolve into separate structures—Coit Tower on Telegraph Hill, the Ferry Building overlooking the ships at the docks, the Clay-Jones on Nob Hill with its radio antenna against the sky like a medieval spire, the Mark Hopkins looking down from its heights in imperial splendor. But the building that caught my eye most compellingly, that seemed to embody in itself the geological and historical forces expressed in the skyline, was a massive tower that rose from a point near the end of the bridge, standing apart from the other skyscrapers in an appropriate climax to this fabulous journey over the water into Camelot.

I was told it was the Telephone Building, and that was all I knew about it for many years, although I used to walk around it and look at it from various perspectives. From the sidewalks in front, I could examine the sculpturings on the walls. From nearby streets it appeared to rise above the old buildings of the South-of-Market District like a structure that belonged to another world. From upper Sansome Street half a mile to the north, it seemed to have a spread-eagle aspect as the sunlight moved across its walls, throwing its fluted piers into sharp relief.

Exploring the downtown area around Union Square, I came across another building that held my eye with its clean vertical lines and its contrasting smooth and textured surfaces. The windows were not set back into the walls with deep sills in the conventional fashion, but were flush with the outer surface and slightly bayed, like hundreds of mirrors differentially reflecting the sunlight at various times of day. I tried to learn the name of the building, but to my surprise it was simply known by its address—450 Sutter.

I remember wondering what manner of men raised these monuments on the city's skyline, what kind of imagination and energy created these towers that seemed to embody the power and excitement of this city at the Western Gate. It was not until many years later, in the course of some research, that I learned that the Telephone Building, 450 Sutter and several others I admired were designed by the same architect.

The more I learned about Timothy Pflueger and his work, the more it seemed to me that his career represented an effort to throw off the copybook architectural styles of the past and to express in vigorous steel and stone the vital essence of this city and its innovative pioneering tradition. Although early in his career he showed a firm grasp of classical styles, he went far beyond the architects who were designing skyscrapers like Gothic cathedrals or Renaissance temples. Pflueger was convinced that a building—like any work of art—could have genuine integrity only if it was a fresh, direct expression of its own time and place, not an attempt to imitate some ancient hallowed tradition.

Unlike most architects of his time, he was not indoctrinated by the dogmas of the classical academies, particulary the Beaux Arts in Paris, then the summit of the art world. He received his training in the streets of San Francisco's Mission District. Along with his five brothers and immigrant German parents he lived in an old house on Guerrero Street and never went beyond high school.

When he was 15 he went to work in the offices of a local architect and within ten years the energetic youngster had designed several buildings including the principal portion of the gleaming white Doric headquarters of Metropolitan Life on Nob Hill (now Cogswell College). He was barely over 30 when, as a partner in the firm of J.R. Miller, he landed the mammoth job of designing the biggest corporate headquarters in the West—the main offices of the Pacific Telephone and Telegraph Company.

On his drawing board he experimented at first with Gothic styles, using the conventional cathedral-like arches and spires. Then he came across a sketch that was setting the architectural world on fire. It was a design which the Finnish architect Eliel Saarinen had entered—unsuccessfully—in a competition for the Chicago Tribune Building.

Saarinen made no attempt to emulate ancient styles but found a style and spirit distinctive to the modern skyscrapers—a soaring, aspiring form that seemed to affirm the limitless possibilities of the new science and technology. It was apparently too unconventional for the judges, who gave it second prize, preferring a Gothic design.

With the Saarinen idea fresh in mind, Pflueger spent a weekend at Fallen Leaf Lake, near Tahoe. Mulling over his problem, he climbed the steep trail to Upper Angora Lake. There, as he looked up at glacier-carved granite walls, the idea came to him—a building that would embody the powerful vertical lines of Saarinen's tower and the clean, uncluttered strength and light-reflecting textures of Sierra granite.

The Telephone Building was finished in 1925, the first architecturally modern skyscraper in San Francisco. Unlike the city's earlier high-rise buildings, it has no horizontal lines; it does not try to disguise its form with cornices, buttresses, or gingerbread but accepts and accentuates its height with sharply ascending piers and tapering stepbacks. The sculptured figures on the facade, suggestive of modern communication, illustrate well Goethe's insight that architecture is "frozen music." A theme first stated in tentative form near the base of the building—a series of stemlike bas-reliefs—is repeated higher up at intervals, each time with greater elaboration until it reaches a climax at the top in a grand architectural fortissimo.

Pflueger may not have been thinking consciously in musical terms, but he had a strong conviction that other fine arts should be involved. The directors' room of the Telephone Buliding had a mural by Arthur Matthews, and Pflueger's commission to design a new home for the San Francisco Stock Exchange enabled him to go even further. His personal charm and enthusiasm overcame the innate conservatism of the financial community, and several notable artists were involved in the building, including San Francisco sculptor Ralph Stackpole and Mexican muralist Diego Rivera.

With 450 Sutter, Pflueger the innovator was the first high-rise architect in the West to take advantage of some of the new possibilities offered by steel-frame construction. Although steel-frame buildings did not need the kind of massive supportive walls that had held up the old masonry buildings, architects had continued to design massive walls simply to conform to tradition. Pflueger eliminated the heavy walls and set the windows at the outer rim of the building, adapting an old San Francisco motif, the Victorian bay window. For better views of the city's magnificent panoramas, he designed the "wrap-around" windows at the building's corners, the exact place that architects had traditionally insisted must show massive strength in masonry. The result was the exterior of contrasting textures. The shining bands of glass, reflecting the sun, alternated with the sculptured Mayan designs between the windows. Light-colored piers extending from the street to the roof gave the building a powerful vertical thrust. Other innovations were a rooftop solarium and basement garage, the first such provision for the automobile in any skyscraper.

With the completion of 450 Sutter, Pflueger had given the city its first totally original high-rise building. But instead of beginning an era, the building closed one. It was finished in early 1930 just a few months after the great stockmarket crash. There was not another high-rise building erected in San Francisco for another two decades of depression and war.

During this period Pflueger was fiercely busy on other projects, working with gargantuan energies until late at night and even filling his bedside note pad with ideas that came to him during sleep. His early work with theaters, beginning with the Art Deco Spanish-style Castro in San Francisco (recently restored to its original grandeur) was climaxed in 1930 by the Paramount in Oakland, an Art Deco classic that is a National Historic Landmark, the home of the Oakland Symphony and Performing Arts. The clean functional lines of the Bay Bridge built in the early 1930s owe much to Pflueger's chairmanship of the board of consulting architects. When the owners of the Mark Hopkins wondered how to bolster the hotel's sagging income, Pflueger suggested and designed a sky-level cocktail lounge, referring to it jokingly as "the top of the Mark." The name stuck. The lounge paid for itself within six months and became a nationally known San Francisco gathering place and landmark.

Pflueger's encouragement of contemporary art found expression in his role as a founder and director of the San Francisco Museum of Modern Art. For similar purposes he organized the popular "Art in Action" exhibit at the 1939-40 World's Fair on Treasure Island, using the talents of Bay Area artists and once again importing Diego Rivera. The exposition's many-columned Federal Building and the breathtaking Court of Pacifica were Pflueger designs. So was the world's first under-park garage at Union Square, which he pushed to completion early in the war by proving to the government that the garage could be used as a bomb shelter. His first big post-war design was the I. Magnin Building on Union Square, sheathed in gleaming white marble, in a unique combination of simplicity and opulence.

Since Pflueger was a gregarious clubman, he had little time for home life, never married, and contined to live in the big old Mission District house where he grew up. One evening in 1946, after his customary swim at the Olympic Club, he dropped dead at the age of 54. Referring to his vast energies and accomplishments, a friend said: "Tim lived two lives in one lifetime."

His brother Milton, 15 years younger, had been a member of the firm since 1929 and a full partner since 1940. With heavy heart, as he notes in this memoir, he took over the firm, determined to carry on his brother's innovative tradition. Among the projects completed by the firm during the subsequent years were the pace-setting civic center across the bay at Richmond, an architecturally unified complex of buildings that served as a focal point for that city's revival after the closing of its World War II shipyards had left it in a state of near collapse. The center was a source of civic pride that sparked the community's renewal.

A dozen Pflueger-designed buildings provided for a vast post-war expansion at the University of San Francisco. The firm's other academic work in recent decades has included a 500-bed hospital for the medical center at the University of California, San Francisco; buildings at San Francisco City College and Stanford; and a complete campus for the College of the Holy Names in the hills behind Oakland.

At Stanford, there were two major problems. One was to rebuild the University's original structures around the Quad, a project that was ingeniously accomplished without significant alteration of the historic Romanesque facades. The other problem was to design new off-Quad buildings in a modern style that would harmonize with the original architecture—a purpose achieved admirably in the Graduate School of Business and the Center for the Biological Sciences.

An award-winning Pflueger design for additions to the California Academy of Sciences in Golden Gate Park was followed by work on several hospitals, climaxed by the Army's $100 million new Walter Reed Hospital in Washington, D.C., which on occasion has housed members of Congress, Supreme Court Justices, Cabinet Members and Presidents.

In the 1980s American architecture stands at the threshold of an era which is potentially even more revolutionary than that inaugurated by Timothy Pflueger six decades earlier in his departure from the Gothic skyscrapers tradition. Once again, established architectural styles are proving inadequate to the demands of the times. The energy crises of the 1970s first dramatized the advent of the need for new ways of thinking about the world around us. The technological abundance based on cheap energy from oil had fostered the delusion that the industrial societies could be independent of the elemental realities that had governed human activities for all but the latest infinitesimal fraction of the human time on earth—the natural community of plants and animals, sunlight, and the cycles of moving air and flowing water.

Revolutionary changes in attitudes do not come overnight, but there are signs of a dawning realization that the resources available to us are not infinite, that humans are part of the cycles of nature and subject to natural limitations, that all forms of human activity, architecture in particular, must learn to coordinate with the natural systems that support all life on earth. Consequently we seem to be on the verge of an era of solar-oriented, energy-conserving architecture that has its own principles, makes its own demands, and challenges the skill and imagination of the entire architectural profession.

Under the direction of John Pflueger, the son, and since 1976 the partner of Milton Pflueger, the firm began its venture into the new environmental architecture with the innovative library at San Jose State University, finished in 1981. The building is not connected to the campus heating and cooling plant but uses its own natural energy system, relying entirely on active and passive solar design.

The same principles were used later in the award-winning California Farm Bureau Federation headquarters in Sacramento, completed in 1980. This time, however, much of the building was underground, keeping the temperature relatively stable in Sacramento's more extreme winter and summer conditions.

In an ingenious arrangement, the rooms are warmed entirely by waste heat from the building's computer center.

A further stage in the evolution of energy-efficient structures has been developed by the Pfluegers in Reno, where the firm has designed a large complex containing a bank headquarters, Performing Arts Center and Fine Arts Museum. Here the solar design is entirely passive, dispensing with collector panels and water tanks. Electricity consumption is kept to a minimum by use of windows, light wells and skylights that provide natural illumination.

It seems fitting that with these buildings the firm given shape by Timothy Pflueger is still on the leading edge of change and that the Pflueger spirit of innovation is finding expression in new directions, not only in the use of solar energy, but in the total design. The buildings of the Reno complex, for example, eloquently reflect in concrete and glass the shapes of the ridges and mesas and monumental rock and slabs of the desert landscapes in the region where that city stands on the edge of the Great Basin.

This book is not a conventional history of a firm. It is primarily a very personal memoir by Milton Pflueger, and it has a special dimension of human warmth because he is a man who is not afraid to express freely his own deeper feelings and thoughts about the people and events he is recalling. He provides a personal perspective on a chapter in the history of San Francisco in which he himself has played a central role. A concluding section by John Pflueger brings the story up to date and relates it to the future of American architecture. In contemplating this vigorous thrust into an era of architecture that is responsive to the natural environment, I must confess to some of the same feelings of excitement that fired my youthful imagination long ago, on those trips across the bay toward that city of fantastic towers on the far shore.

PREFACE

These are some reflections on the unfinished story of Pflueger Architects, a story of my brother Timothy L. Pflueger, myself, and my son, John.

Born and raised in San Francisco, here we have practiced our profession for more than 75 years; the practice is not about to stop, hence "unfinished."

The writing was suggested by John in late 1976. As it was true that only I could preserve a record of many facts and circumstances of our history, the task quickly proved most welcome in times of repose. Although not a writer, I became quite vain and possessive. The reflections and words are therefore mine alone, written with one primary concern, a selfish one. In future years, if memory is not quite sharp, I will turn these pages and live again with those who made it all possible.

Now, in 1983, when printing of these recollections seems probable, I think how long ago it was that the writing of these recollections began, the lapses that occurred in these years and their causes. The chronology:

July 1976	Start
October 1977	Finish—Chapter 23
December 1977.	"Afterthoughts I"
December 1980	"Afterthoughts II"
July 1981	"And Now"
1984	John's Chapter

The lapse of three years between Afterthoughts I and Afterthoughts II was primarily due to my diminishing interest, a wonder of the purpose and value. Also, the consideration of moving our office was time consuming; but the actual perusal of memorabilia re-instigated the nostalgia and what I felt was certainly to be my last bit—"Afterthoughts II."

So it stood. Never at any time did I wish to bring things up-to-date, preferring to leave the thoughts and words as I felt at the time of first writing.

Once more though, in 1981, an event led to still another chapter—"And Now."

In September 1981, there came the impetus. John and I were talking at length with Harold Gilliam at the FAMILY FARM in Woodside, Harold and his work having been the subject of special events at THE FARM. In the course of the conversation my writing adventure was mentioned. Harold expressed interest, and some time later read the manuscript, made the most kind and thoughtful suggestions, rekindling the pride in our heritage and record. With his great knowledge of environmental preservation and its influence on design, he was extremely interested in John's philosophy and suggested an account by John of recent years as a two-generation counterpoint. John's final chapter, written despite the press of business, is the result.

In short, were it not for the encouragement by Harold, this book would not be.

March 1983

Milton T. Pflueger

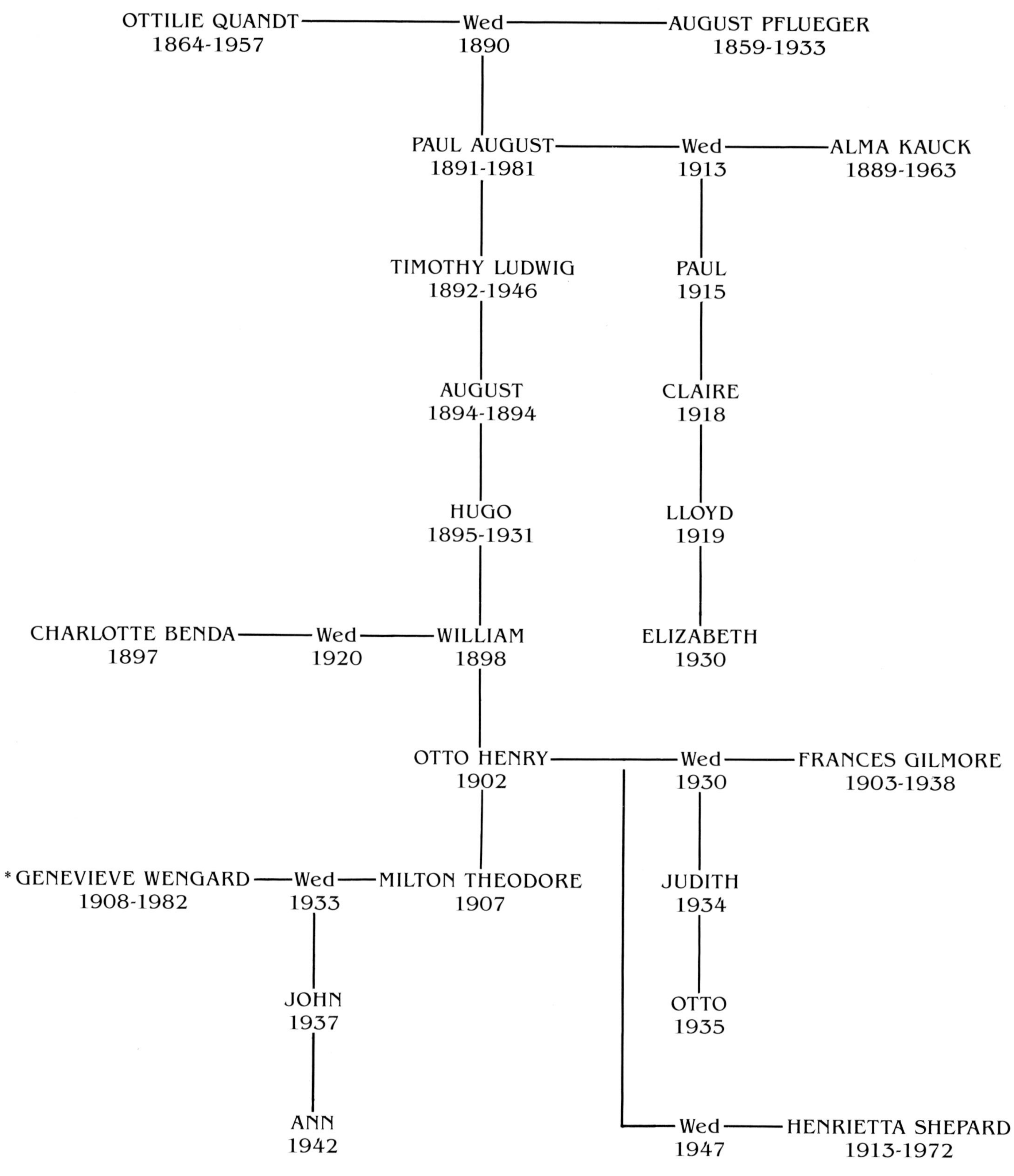

*Now, at the time of printing, the author said:
Let us here insert the year 1982, thus marking the end of an earthly life of purest beauty.
Make no changes in the text of the book.
As it was at the time of writing, neither can I now find words.

INTRODUCTION

My oldest brother Paul, when asked how it was that all the Pfluegers boys "turned out so well" (it was so put, at times), always replied, "think only of our mother and father." I cannot go back farther in heritage than my mother's father, who visited us every Sunday noon for our dinner after he had been to Church (one different from that to which we all went) and after he had stopped for a "schnapps" on his walk to our house. He lived to 90 years, my mother to 93, and my father to 74.

Mother's three brothers and her sister all emigrated from Germany and resided in California. The family remained very close and uncles, aunts, cousins, nieces and nephews seemed innumerable.

Of my father's ancestors and immediate family I only know of his birthplace, my brother Otto having taken a picture of the house in Egringen, Germany, a town across the Rhine and not far from Basel, Switzerland. Paul and Tim traced other Pfluegers in our country but were unable to establish a family connection. The Pfluegers of the famous fishing reel were of course among those contacted, but again to no conclusions. It would be strange I suppose if there was no ancestral connection with Pfluegers of our land (Pflügers originally, I was told), but the matter, interesting though it may be, rests.

Our mother and father both emigrated at very early ages, met and married in Los Angeles in 1890 and soon thereafter moved to San Francisco, where in the Mission District all the boys were born.

Our father was a merchant tailor. The older children all worked at early ages; to keep the family going was not at all easy—hard work was set as the example and this was never to be forgotten. My father's shop was on the first floor of our home on Guerrero Street. Just above was the "parlor" with its piano where we all practiced our lessons. If we hit a wrong note we heard an immediate knock through the floor below. His ear was good and he also had a strong bass voice. He wrote poetry, but he was stern and strict. It was often my mother's task to speak up and protect her boys from his ruler. She was gentle and loving and very proud of her boys who, in her thoughts, could do no wrong.

So it was that Paul's answer never changed, and if there is something a bit uncommon in that six boys "did well," we know whence it came.

I would like to tell of all my brothers, their accomplishments, their help to the little kid brother who came along when my mother was 43 and my father 48. If at all, that should have been done long ago. We were all too busy and now I'll try only to tell something about one of the segments of the family and how it goes on.

This is not historical. History, however short its time frame, denotes to me research, references and study. Several times I have started to search and classify. The wealth of material is so great that if I once started on such a course, there would be no way to stop, or to select in proper perspective. That requires great concentration and patience, which in truth I no longer have.

Nothing, however, is imaginative. What is written is fact, written in the spirit of spontaneity and sure memory.

1. BIRTHPLACE OF AUGUST PFLUEGER IN EGRINGEN, Germany, (Otto Pflueger). After completing his internship in San Francisco, Otto Pflueger had a residency of several years at New York Memorial Hospital. He was then given the present of an extended European study tour by his brother Tim, during which Otto tried to find some information about ancestors. Residents in Egringen pointed out the family home and he took this picture.

Timothy

2. A luncheon given by Tim at the FAMILY City Club for the engineers and architects of the San Francisco-Oakland Bay Bridge. Starting at upper left around the table: C.S. Proctor—Construction Engineer; Leon Moisseff—Construction Engineer; Ralph Modjeski—Construction Engineer; Charles H. Purcell—Chief Engineer; Timothy L. Pflueger—Chairman, Consulting Board of Architects; Leland W. Cutler—Financial Advisor; Unrecognized; Glenn B. Woodruff—Engineer of Design; H.J. Brunnier—Construction Engineer; Unrecognized; Unrecognized; Lloyd W. Dinkelspiel—Attorney; John J. Donovan—Consulting Board of Architects; Charles E. Andrew—Bridge Engineer; Charles Derleth—Consulting Engineer; Arthur Brown, Jr.—Consulting Board of Architects.

These photographs of Timothy were taken by Ansel Adams in 1940.

Milton

Milton and John

THE EARLY YEARS OF TIMOTHY PFLUEGER

What motivated Tim to be an Architect? I cannot recall his ever speaking directly to the point, but surely it was predestined, for I can think of no other life than architecture that could have provided for him an equal sense of satisfaction and accomplishment. As a boy he worked at a picture-framing shop. He drew and painted beautifully at an early age. He found a position as an apprentice in Miller and Colmesnil's architectural office while going to evening high school, and soon proved his talent.

In 1912, when only 20 years of age, his employer J.R. Miller had him design a Catholic Church, Our Lady of the Wayside in Portola Valley. He worked on the first stages of the Metropolitan Life Insurance Company Headquarters, which he in later years added to stage by stage. During these early years he was fortunate in having J.R. Miller as his employer, for the opportunities he enjoyed were exceptional.

In World War I, as a civilian with the Army Corps of Engineers, he worked in Washington and in Puerto Rico, where he designed training camp facilities. His letters and pictures from Puerto Rico were most revealing, indicating his liking of the people and the country, as well as his work, where his contacts with the Fathers of the Church led to mutual respect and personal relationships. Perhaps this was due in a sense to his great regard for the dynamic young priest, Father George Lacombe, the Pastor at Our Lady of the Wayside Church, his earliest client contact.

Directly adjoining that church property is the 100-acre FAMILY FARM, the country home of the San Francisco men's club, where on particular weekends the members gather and dedicate their time ". . . to Music and Laughter, to Folly and to Truth, to Peace and Hope, and to that love of man for man which makes the hard path easy and the crooked way straight . . ." (from the Peroration of Edward H. Hamilton, First Father of THE FAMILY, on the dedication of THE FAMILY at its city home in 1902).

THE FAMILY was founded in April, 1902, by 36 men—27 of them members or former members of the Bohemian Club, started some thirty years earlier. From its first "home" at Montgomery and Commercial Streets, it moved to Post Street, and after the earthquake to Franklin and Clay. Its present Italian Renaissance structure at Bush and Powell was built in 1909.

Just a few years after Tim's return from the war, THE FAMILY became his haven as did the Bohemian and Olympic Clubs.

The Clubs provided his hours of play. A bachelor, he received there the friendship and relaxation needed from a hard work schedule.

We brothers were all very close, being together almost all of our years in San Francisco. I know that in my years with Tim, hardly a day passed that he did not talk with Paul. Paul and Timothy, less than two years apart in age, of completely different temperaments and talents; the first marrying early and lovingly devoted to family, the second never marrying, yet conferring with and advising each other throughout the years.

With twenty-five years of banking, then almost another fifty years in the investment business, Paul was Tim's confidante in all things, and he has been that to all his brothers. As their first son, our parents named him well, and their second son Timothy equally as well. The Biblical connotation was of course intended and it never faltered. Later, given names for the sons took a turn toward the poetic and dramatic form, the reason for which I never heard. Church and Sunday School nevertheless continued unabated for all the boys.

I wonder though as I think of it, just how long Hugo continued in the tradition. He, much more than any other, kicked over the traces. He thought nothing of putting a sling on his right arm on the way to school, or any other excuse to avoid lessons. Richard "Dickie" Faulkner, the principal at Horace Mann Grammar School, at Valencia and 22nd Streets, just a block from our home on Guerrero Street, spent many an afternoon in our father's tailor shop, and while I heard much general conversation between two good friends, "Hug" was a particular subject of the conversation quite often.

He seemed tough; let's face it, Hug was tough, but the ice cream cones and chocolate eclairs he brought to his kid brother are among my earliest and fondest memories; and when I first brought Gen home and introduced her to my family (a night which she says "terrified" her), it was he who said the next morning, "She's all right, kid!" I am sorry that my children never knew their father's brother Hugo, nor their father's father.

Paul and Bill married at early years; Hugo was an engineer in the merchant marine; Otto, the surgeon (the only one whose formal education went beyond high school) was at the University, medical school, and in Europe. From my birth in 1907 until I married in 1933 I lived with my parents, as did Tim from his birth until his death. So it was I that had the longest "at home" time with Tim, and was with him in his office from 1929 until 1946, the year of his untimely death.

In my four plus years (1925-1929) at Bakewell & Brown, Tim allowed me to visit his jobs and his office, so that even then he was not out of my picture. Fifteen years age difference, half a generation, but never enough to the point that I was unaware of his greatness and his life. How fortunate could one be. Much more so had he only lived to an expected normal life span, rather than age 54. But what was accomplished in those years! If I can bring his work and play into focus to even a minor degree, it is more than I hope for.

Close friends, countless as they were, gave zest and meaning to his work and every hour of his life. I was privileged to know his friends and to count them as my friends.

Florence M. McAuliffe (Mac) of Heller, Ehrman, White & McAuliffe, the prestigious law firm, and William H. McCarthy, the former Postmaster of San Francisco, were perhaps the most personal men friends of all. Mac also never married, and this permitted many occasions of play at the Clubs and elsewhere. Billy, perhaps the greatest toastmaster of those or any other days, always presided at the monthly dinners of the members of the Olympic Club Locker Room 328. My brother Otto and I were also in the Room and can vouch for the unmatched parties that a group of close, fun-loving men can have.

Bill and Rita McCarthy had a country place in Ben Lomond. Occasionally on a late Friday afternoon, they would pick up Tim's lady friend and companion of 20 years, Alice Plagemann, then Tim, and drive to the country for a quiet weekend. These respites were good, although yellow pads filled with job notes and sketches would be brought back on Sunday. We did a firehouse in Ben Lomond for Bill and his friends. In appreciation they presented Tim the Chief's fire helmet (which I still have) and he enjoyed donning it while strolling at the FAMILY FARM and the Bohemian Grove.

Rarely, I will concede, but seemingly in the middle of the night at home, a phone call from pals visiting from distant places would inquire if he could not, right then, "go out," and the answer was "surely" more often than "no, sorry." Such recollections bring smiles, also wonder at the boundless energy and the full life.

Let me not forget particular friends such as Larry Harris, who wrote the "Damnedest Finest Ruins" after the '06 quake and who gave so much of his talents to THE FAMILY; Sidney Ehrman, "Uncle Sidney" of the great law firm; Louis Stewart , Leland Cutler, the prime instigator of the '39 and '40 Exposition; Roy Folger, the inimitable story teller; Harold Faulkner, an early friend from Mission Evening High School; Billy Smith who produced club shows in addition to his Title Insurance duties, and Vincent Duffey, the lighting expert whose talents made club shows experiences never to be forgotten. I remember the rededication in 1938 after we remodelled THE FAMILY City Club at Bush and Powell, I was sitting next to Vin; a particular lighting effect threw tree shadows upon the new panelled ceiling. I said something like "look at that great ceiling"; Vin laughed uproariously, and kindly chided me for not remarking on the lighting which made it all so vivid. I should not stop about great friends but there would be no ending, so I bow my head to the hundreds who will never be forgotten.

In the office, I am still using the same ancient office desk that Tim used throughout his life, having hoped, I suppose, that thereby more of Tim would continue to rub off on me. Thinking now of Vin Duffey reminds me that when going through the shallow desk drawer I found a letter to Tim from Vin. Through the years, in one place or another, many notes, letters and memos have been found, but I particularly like this one (even though Vin slipped in omitting Tim's role in the Bay Bridge, the starting point in his tale!). Here it is, word for word.

VINCENT E. DUFFEY

San Francisco
December 10, 1945

Dear Tim:

At the risk of boring you, I simply must tell you an amusing story on both you and myself:

A short time ago friends of mine from the East—Dr. Hulbert and his wife—arrived in town for a few days. I lunched with them at the St. Francis, where they were staying, after which I took them on a sightseeing trip around San Francisco and environs. As we were returning to town over the Bay Bridge, the doctor exclaimed in delight as he glimpsed the Telephone Building, beautifully silhouetted in the autumnal twilight. 'What a magnificent edifice! I had no idea you had such buildings in San Francisco. Who was the architect?' I mentioned your name and he asked, 'An eastern man, of course?' I smiled!

Off the ramp, I drove to Nob Hill and we went to the Top of the Mark for cocktails. It was one of those splendid, crystalline evenings and they were enchanted. After drinking deeply of the vistas, we settled down at a table to do likewise with bourbon. It was then that Mrs. Hulbert became fully aware of your room '. . . the most beautiful place of its kind in the world! Who was the architect?' 'The same man who did the Telephone Building,' I answered, 'Tim Pflueger, no less.' And with a pride of friendship, enhanced by the second and third drink, I gave them what I think was a good Profile of you. (No, I didn't mention Eddy Street or Westwood Village!) Bubbling over with enthusiasm, I then took them over to the Circus Room at the Fairmont to show off your other Nob Hill saloon. I'll bet your ears were burning that night.

A day or two later I joined them at the St. Francis for cocktails. We gathered in the Orchid Room and they were full of their doings in San Francisco. Doc had had luncheon at the Stock Exchange Club '. . . and to my amazement, I learned that *your* Mr. Pflueger had been the architect.' His host had also hiked him around and showed him the Pine Street facade. We spoke of Stackpole's sculptures and I told them of the dedicatory ceremonies on that rainy New Year's Eve. I recounted that the direction and lighting was by one Vin Duffey. Hell, I had to get into the act somehow! The Doc nodded and said he remembered that I had somewhat of a reputation for lighting. 'In fact, I was talking about you last night. Our friends, the Lorands, took us to the Bal Tabarin. The lighting and the room was so unique that I ventured the opinion that it was your work. Yes?' 'No,' I answered, 'the Pflueger guy did that too!' (Did I see a slight gleam of suspicion in the Doc's eyes that I was pulling his leg?)

After a couple of drinks came the query that I had been anticipating! 'Who was the genius that created this most unusual cocktail lounge?' Well, damned if I was going to be sucked in on that one. I scratched my head and murmured: 'His name seems to have escaped me.' But the avid doctor beckoned to a captain and repeated his question. When he heard the reply, 'Mr. Timothy L. Pflueger,' the Doc frowned incredulously and barked, 'My God, is the man twins?'

Presently it was time to depart for the Sea Cliff, where we had all been invited for dinner. I took them through the subway to the Union Square Garage, where I had parked my car. Well, when they got a look at that underground maze, the Doc was all agog. He poked around and did everything but slide down the pole to the lower decks. He even recalled reading in a Chicago paper, en route to the Coast, that Detroit was planning such a garage patterned on this very one. 'Why in hell don't we have things like this in New York?' Then, with a touch of a threat in his voice, he asked, 'And who in hell was the architect for this?' 'Pflueger,' I cried. And winced as he muttered, 'You know, Vin, I think you've turned into a lying bastard! To keep my reputation for veracity inviolate, I had to take them up to the monument and show them your name chiseled into the gleaming white shaft.

They left the following evening on the Lark for Los Angeles. I had the doctor up to THE FAMILY for a quick drink before train time. I'm most sorry that you weren't there, Tim, not only so that you could have met him, but also to prove that you're not a legend or a corporation. He liked the Club, but I suspect he had become wary because, strangely enough, he didn't inquire as to the architect!

As we left THE FAMILY and walked down Powell Street, he paused for a moment and contemplated your imposing 450 Sutter Building. Then he cocked an eyebrow in my direction and I smilingly nodded a mute affirmation of his unspoken sixty-four-dollar question. He shook his head in bewilderment as we continued on to his hotel.

Well, that's the story of the Hulberts. I think it's rather amusing—and yet, I wonder. For when they pulled out on the Lark, I fear a long and delightful friendship came to an end. I could almost hear them talking in their compartment after they left me: 'Poor old Vin! What do you suppose it is—an early senility, or delusions of grandeur?' Now that I think about it, I can hardly blame them!

As ever,
/s/ VIN

P.S. Gad, suppose I had shown them all of your stuff!!''

I will not leave THE FAMILY without a bit more on the FAMILY FARM at Woodside. This redwood grove, with its meandering creek and "camps" for members numbering from several to twenty or more, was one of Tim's great loves. He not only enjoyed its set weekends with the programmed shows but every bit as much those other occasions when he, with a friend or two or three, would suddenly say "let's go down and spend the night at the Farm." It held a fascination, with but a companion or two, that only a place of special natural beauty could hold. He jealously guarded the natural beauties as Farm Committee Chairman for many years and when he designed needed improvements such as camp additions, the outdoor dining area, or the Tavern, they were done with extreme sensitivity to natural preservation and traditional simplicity. I recall the trunks of redwoods through the Tavern kitchen, the Tavern, its bar looking to the opposite creek bank with trees and their shadows, sunlight filtering; the outdoor bar the same, and the whole with its natural materials fitting so beautifully into place. It was fun to work for Tim on this Tavern and see it being built in 1931, and then for me to add a small "Poker Room," many years later.

Those who have lain on the soft needled ground with log back-rests and gazed up at the redwoods, seen the "lace of a thousand trees," heard soft music by the hidden talented Children, know "what more for a man than these." . . . From Waldemar Young's words to Uda Waldrop's "Song of the Night," for the "Family Play" of 1927.

3. METROPOLITAN LIFE INSURANCE COMPANY, San Francisco, First Unit 1909 (Gabriel Moulin) J.R. Miller. J.R. Miller initiated the Metropolitan Life Insurance connection which continued for many years through additions and alterations until completion of the San Francisco Headquarters.

4. METROPOLITAN LIFE INSURANCE COMPANY, Main Facade 1919 (Gabriel Moulin). Miller & Pflueger, by Timothy Pflueger.

5. METROPOLITAN LIFE INSURANCE COMPANY, Completion 1930 (Gabriel Moulin). Miller & Pflueger, by Timothy Pflueger.

THE ARTS AND ARTISTS

The days were too short, but Tim found time to be one of the founders of the San Francisco Museum of Modern Art and persuaded his good friend W.W. Crocker to serve as President. Tim's association with the San Francisco Art Institute was one of many years. He designed the sets and helped produce the annual Parilias given for the benefit of the Institute, gala parties at the Civic Auditorium never to be forgotten. He induced friends to become patrons and lovers of art. He was the Director of Art for the Golden Gate Exposition. His "Art in Action" at the Exposition exposed the artists to the public as no other event before or since. He raised funds to again bring Diego Rivera from Mexico to paint a monumental fresco, later given to City College of San Francisco, where we installed it years later in the Auditorium Lobby.

Artists were his friends, and he theirs. Respect, admiration and appreciation bound them strongly; throughout his career their work was integrated into his to the greatest degree possible. He was able to convince his clients of the beauty and value of this marriage.

Tim was on the Board of Directors of the San Francisco Art Institute from 1930 until his death in 1946. He served as President from 1932 through 1937, and upon his retirement from the Presidency there was a presentation to him of two large leather folios, each containing forty matted originals. Eighty fine artists thereby expressed their appreciation to Tim, and gave him the most personal manifestation of their friendship.

Too few years remained for Tim to savor this treasure. I have been given the years, and as I look at the drawings, the paintings, the etchings, the artists' names I see weave a lifetime thread of memories.

At the age of seventeen, in early 1925, as I started in the office of Bakewell & Brown, one of the jobs in the office was the California School of Fine Arts, later the San Francisco Art Institute, on Chestnut Street. Lee Randolph and Spencer Macky, Directors of the School, were frequently in the office. I'd see them, poring over the plans of the School with Arthur Brown and others, and now their art is included in the folios I view, fifty and more years later.

Ralph Stackpole, with his sparkling eyes, full of life and ideas; I see him in his studio yard on Telegraph Hill, or here in our office where he would take a small white pad, draw quickly a face or a figure with a few pure, sure lines, tear off the page and hand it to me, pages which tragically I cannot find. We have his small scale plaster models of the center anchorage of the Bay Bridge, heroic figures straining to anchor the suspension cables. Why did Tim not take the thought all the way? It would not distract the pilots guiding the ships through the Bay—or would it? I do not remember the particulars and will not presume. I watched Ralph, using hammer and chisel, high on the scaffolds around the Stock Exchange sculptures, as did so many others. Was this one of the "inspirations" for the *"Art in Action"* at the '39-'40 Exposition? (See Chapter 6.)

And if Tim had help in enticing Diego Rivera to San Francisco to do the Stock Exchange fresco, and he must have, then surely it was Ralph along with the eminent surgeon Leo Eloesser, both being friends of Rivera. It was Eloesser who went to Spain during the Franco Revolution, writing brief postcards such as "Tim, you should be here."

I recall Ralph's letters from France. Some few years after Tim's death, Ralph and his French-born wife returned to her family home, there to farm and raise chickens, but Ralph never lost his interest in matters such as monuments on the island in our Bay. And I think of Ralph's son Peter Stackpole, who as a young man worked in our office for a short time. As one of Life magazine's first photographers, he so dramatically portrayed the building of the Bay Bridge.

I see Bob Howard's very sensitive drawing with his warm words to Tim. How could one do so many things, and all so well. He painted on wood panels for the Stock Exchange Club, where his wife Adeline Kent also contributed sculpture. He sculptured not only the walls of the Paramount Theater auditorium but also the "dancing girls" in the Lobby. His "Whales" feature the Court of the Academy of Sciences, and his "Phoenix" enhances our Student Center at the University of San Francisco. Bob's brother Henry, an architect, worked for a short while in our office, in my very early years. Their father was John Galen Howard, the famous University of California architect.

Lucien Labaudt—in these later years when once or twice I have met and conversed with Eric Hoffer I have been struck not only by the physical similarity, but by the same quality of zest—restlessness—inquisitiveness—an awareness of everything that is going on. Lucien—who lost his life on assignment as an artist capturing the emotion of War for Life magazine. What an artist—what a man! Tim spoke at the christening of the "Lucien Labaudt," a Liberty ship, and I can see them, where they are now, bear-hugging each other.

The Bruton sisters, Helen, Esther and Margaret—each a gifted artist. When an artist conceives, the sketches, the studies, the working by the hands, be it graphic or otherwise, accompany the mental process. It is something special to see these studies even after the fact, but if one is privileged to be present at their making, that is something very special. This comes to mind whenever I glance with appreciation at the many "studies" or "samples" of art which we are fortunate to have in the office. I saw many being done, and just a glance now brings joyful memories. One sample is on a 12" x 8" piece of hardboard, made by Helen Bruton for the murals she executed in the Circus Room of the Fairmont Hotel. The Bruton sisters were particular favorites of Tim, and to see a representation of their fine art in the folios recalls the significant contributions they made to Tim's work, among which was "The Peacemakers," the huge mural in the Court of the Pacific at the '39-'40 Exposition.

Sargent Johnson—who sculpted the models for the grand cast-in-place concrete frieze at the Athletic Field of our George Washington High School. Interestingly, it was Benny Bufano to whom Tim first talked regarding this work. To my knowledge this architect-artist collaboration was the single instance in Tim's career which was not realized. Were they each too strong in conviction to agree on whatever the issue might have been? I have no recollections of another answer. A red granite "Cat" by Sargent Johnson has a particular niche in our home.

Charles Stafford Duncan did a fine mural in the Paramount Theater and in my home we enjoy the 24 inch square "sample" he made as a study for the mural. Stafford was the art director for McCann, Erickson as I remember.

Otis Oldfield, who added a facet of his art to the Stock Exchange Club, was small in stature, great in ability. He was among the many artists whom Tim brought into THE FAMILY, among them Moya del Pino, Ralph Stackpole, Rinaldo Cuneo, Lucien Labaudt and Tony Sotomayor. Their work is in the folios, as well as gracing the City Home of THE FAMILY.

Victor Arnautoff I see, doing frescoes at our George Washington High School in the very early '30s, and I see a William Gaw, a George Post, a Dong Kingman, a Jacques Schneir, a Ruth Cravath and so many more.

Why only now am I setting these thoughts down? Unlike Tim, who somehow found time for all things, living not one but many lives, I had time for work only after Tim's death. We were so busy that I did not have time for recollections, only to continue and follow Tim with the work of architecture. That in itself seemed all I could do. Not throughout all the years though. I came to play as well, and those times of play are very fresh in mind. Tim once wrote me while flying East: "Milt, I think you take our work too seriously. You must learn to relax and play." I did, am glad, and am thankful for such a great teacher in all things.

So these folios, with the gifts of art from so many friends, afford not only great pleasure in the viewing of them, but also evoke memories for all time. One can imagine what this commemorative gift from his friends meant to Tim.

6. CLAUS SPRECKELS BUILDING, San Francisco, circa 1906. In the 1906 earthquake and fire in San Francisco some prominent buildings were under construction, some badly damaged and rebuilt, or, of course, in some instances, so badly destroyed that the completion or rebuilding was impossible (as was the case with the City Hall which subsequently became the subject of scandal due to improper design and/or materials).

In our files of J.R. Miller's work in that period we have found interesting examples, one of which is the Claus Spreckels Building located at the southwest corner of Third and Market streets. The upper illustration is his rendering of the lower floors of this structure. The illustration on the left is a photo after completion.

Some years ago the exterior of this building was completely remodeled by another architectural firm. Unfortunately, the result retains little of the character and charm of the original design.

7. *QUICK STUDY SKETCHES, early 1920s.*

These four sketches, made in the office in the very early 1920s, illustrate the search that was going on in our office, (and without question, in many offices across our land) for an expression suitable to the skyscraper. The studies range from stylistic to the dominant verticality and dominant horizontality.

Our Pacific Telephone & Telegraph Headquarters Building and 450 Sutter, described and illustrated in the following chapter, were completed in 1925 and in early 1930 respectively. Each, in its time, was a clear "first".

However, even prior to the studies on the Telephone Building, these sketches clearly indicate the thought process, the search for an expression free of bondage to the past. (It is also interesting to note that some ten years hence, in 1932, William Lescaze, of Howe and Lescaze, employed the dominant horizontal theme in the Philadelphia Savings Fund Society Building, a project which then received wide acclaim).

It is not unfair to say that the designs of many of our newer skyscrapers lack sensitivity and inspiration; our profession might well start afresh, as did Tim in the early 1920s.

8. CASTRO THEATER, San Francisco, 1921 (drawing: Timothy Pflueger). The Nasser brothers, early theater owners in San Francisco, commissioned Timothy Pflueger to do this theater when he was 28 years of age. Many more theaters for the Nassers and others were done by the firm in the years to come, and this was the start.

THE 1920s

On Tim's return after the war to San Francisco, he became J.R. Miller's partner, this lasting until J.R.'s retirement, a year or two before his death in the early '30s.

In the early '20s, theaters for the Nasser Brothers, T & D Enterprises and other clients were a large part of Tim's work. They were of all styles; the Castro the first, with its Spanish influence, the Alhambra, its name is enough, Tulare, Chico, Oroville and many others; in a few years, the El Rey, the Alameda in the more modern tone, culminating in 1929 with undoubtedly one of three great movie-stage theaters in the country, the Paramount in Oakland, now the home of the Oakland Symphony and the Performing Arts. This 3,600 seat theater, a masterpiece of Art Deco, must be seen to be believed. More on this later.

In the 1920s Tim designed two of San Francisco's earliest "skyscrapers": the Headquarters for the Pacific Telephone and Telegraph Company, completed in 1925; and the Medical Building, known simply as 450 Sutter, completed in early 1930.

The Eliel Saarinen submission in the 1922 Chicago Tribune competition undoubtedly inspired the design of the Telephone Building. The Saarinen design placed second to Raymond Hood's conventional Gothic adaptation, which was built.

The Tribune competition was most remarkable in that it brought forth, in the Saarinen design, a new expression of architecture, an expression void of past bondage, setting back as it rose to the sky, suitable as nothing before for the skyscraper. The theme was embraced by the architectural world. Although greatly different in mass, solidity and proportion, the Telephone Building was a descendant of the Saarinen Tribune style and one of the first modern skyscrapers in the nation.

It was not until the later '20s that Tim made his greatest contribution to San Francisco's skyline. With 450 Sutter the exhilaration that comes with sure awareness, insight and creativity bursts forth in every aspect. Bay windows, even at corners where heretofore mass was the normal design requisite, thin exterior curtain walls with flush windows, tapestried Mayan terra cotta spandrels in the plane of the bay windows. Soaring unbroken to the very roof, an undulating series of splayed piers, bayed windows and tapestried spandrels, there is a strength and beauty unequalled in the previous eclectic work of the affluent '20s, here in San Francisco, or for that matter, in our country. Completed in early 1930, it was a clear first: a call to new thinking, based upon logic, reason and emotion. It remains an example of architecture at its finest.

9. PACIFIC TELEPHONE AND TELEGRAPH COMPANY, San Francisco, 1925 (Hugh Ferriss). This rendering of the Main Facade by Hugh Ferriss, the master of architectural delineation, beautifully depicts the soaring quality and the style of decoration, symbolic of communication components.

10. PACIFIC TELEPHONE AND TELEGRAPH COMPANY, 1925 (Gabriel Moulin).Looking northwest from South of Market Street to the graceful tower.

11. P.T. & T., (Gabriel Moulin). View from the corner of Market and New Montgomery streets.

12. P.T. & T., (Gabriel Moulin). The one-eighth inch scale model superimposed into its actual place.

13. P.T. & T., 1925 (Gabriel Moulin). At parapet, the closing notes of the "grand architectural fortissimo."

14. P.T. & T., (Gabriel Moulin). The beginning, with the opening notes of a theme which will repeat time and again on the tower—as Harold Gilliam writes in his "THE FACE OF SAN FRANCISCO"—"each time with greater elaboration until it reaches a climax at the top in a grand architectural fortissimo."

15. P.T. & T., 1925 (Gabriel Moulin). From the clefts of the highest pinnacle, the American eagles are fiercely watchful over their domain. (In some recent year, blank panels have taken their place. Surely, weather damaged they may have been, but just as the terra cotta facing and other decorations were repaired and preserved, why was the same not done with these proud symbolic creatures?)

16. P.T. & T. (Gabriel Moulin). Model of the eagle photographed in the terra cotta manufacturing plant of Gladding, McBean & Company.

17. P.T. & T. (Gabriel Moulin). Detail nearing the uppermost pinnacle.

18. 450 SUTTER, San Francisco, 1930 (Gabriel Moulin). Sutter Street view. Windows wrapped around all corners, undulating verticals to the very roof, slightly splayed windows and tapestried spandrels in same plane.

19. 450 SUTTER, 1930 (Phil Palmer). The question is often asked—why Mayan? The obvious answer—why not Mayan? Is it not ideally appropriate for a deeply modelled, textured surface, particularly on the exterior spandrels, which are thereby 'grayed' in contrast to the smooth vertical piers?

A further insight! Tim always had an affinity for all Indian culture and also for the countries across the Pacific. When speaking of architectural style for the G.G.I.E. he said "It's too damn bad we didn't have the Oriental influence on the coast instead of the European."

While I was still in school, Tim took me to Felix Atherton's model shop where I saw the Telephone Building being "built," and I entered Tim's office as 450 was being constructed. (Before 450 was started, and after the Synagogue on the site was razed, at lunch time I would meet a friend at the empty lot and play catch, "keeping in shape" for our Sunday semi-pro ball game; baseball was not far from uppermost in my mind in that period, our team winning the "B" League one year and the "A" League the very next year!)

450 Sutter was the end of an era, not the beginning. The stock market crash—a few months before 450's completion—the Depression, and World War II resulted in no large downtown buildings for a quarter of a century.

In 1924, upon graduation from High School, I was ready to enter the University as a step in my endeavor to enter Tim's world, but he advised otherwise. He was of the opinion that the architectural schools were not giving sufficient consideration to new, fresh thinking, and were overly traditional.

Thinking it unwise that I enter his office at the time, he obtained an interview for me at Bakewell & Brown, and John Bakewell was good enough to see me. I became an "office boy-apprentice" in that fine office. It was strange that Tim selected a firm so firmly committed to the classic tradition. This was very wise however, for that was an exceptional office, peopled not only by John Bakewell and the great classic genius Arthur Brown, but other fine architects such as Ernest Weihe, Ed Frick, John Bauer, Larry Kruse and others, all of whom were most considerate and helpful to a young 17 year old. They set me on the track, starting me with the San Francisco Architectural Club with its Beaux Arts Institute ateliers, evening classes, private tutelage and schooling which I feel sure was unavailable at most universities. The training was similar to the very early training of Tim, who had been a very active leader in the Architectural Club.

The training in the '20s at Bakewell & Brown and the San Francisco Architectural Club should not be so briefly dismissed, so a few more fond recollections will be noted.

When my stint as office boy was thought sufficient, and I went on as a junior draftsman, I was followed by John McGilvray III. John, always "Jack" to me, was of the McGilvray Granite family, and the McGilvray-Raymond granite was the material for so many of our finest buildings.

20. 450 SUTTER, 1930 (Gabriel Moulin). Entrance lobby.

21. 450 SUTTER, (Gabriel Moulin). Elevator lobby.

Jack's Uncle Jack was the head of the company and a frequent visitor to the office, and anyone familiar with the early history of the Shrine Hospital would know the Hospital and its origin was of his doing. As I think of "my" Shrine Hospital, it again occurs to me that the thread of my life never did snap.

Jack and I became close friends, working together at the office and at the Club atelier. He was a great pool and billiard player and we spent many hours over the tables at the Club, a change from the charettes on the Beaux Arts Institute problems. We won a few "mentions" along the way, but there is one thing I do remember well. With almost every issue of the Institute Bulletin there seemed to be a photograph of a prize award to Eero Saarinen who I believe was then at Harvard. He of course was of a highly gifted family, and his later meteoric career (cut short at its height) was no surprise to those who knew his early work at school.

Jack McGilvray did not pursue architecture, but went into the business world where his architectural background was certainly of value.

Ernest Born—his work at the Club atelier was inspiring to all, designing and rendering as few men can. To have known Ernest all these years as a good friend has been a stroke of great fortune.

There were so many fine things about the San Francisco Architectural Club in those years. Not only because of our atelier patrons (most of Ecole des Beaux Arts training, to be sure) but the many related classes with exceptional instructors.

One of my structural engineering instructors was R.S. Chew, who had tutored Tim some twenty years before. Another was Jack Sly, who worked in the office of C.H. Snyder, the consultant engineer for most of Bakewell & Brown's work (and 450 Sutter for Tim). Still another young engineer in Snyder's office was Michael Pregnoff, later practicing as Pregnoff and Mathieu, and doing work for our office. A young engineer in Pregnoff and Mathieu's office, Ken Beebe, is now doing much of our consulting work as PMB (Pregnoff, Mathieu and Beebe). To me, this thread, an unbroken skein of nearly seventy years, is quite remarkable.

22. PACIFIC EDGEWATER CLUB, San Francisco, 1927 (Hugh Ferriss). The design for a social club on Point Lobos, the dramatic site overlooking the Pacific. In 1927 this was a dream of certain San Franciscans, a dream unfulfilled because of the Crash in 1929. The original of this Hugh Ferriss rendering and others of this master rank high in the treasures of Pflueger Architects.

The men at Bakewell & Brown found time to help the youngster, to let him work on his own in the office at night, to criticize his atelier work; in general they were the most kindly people. I was fortunate in being present when such projects as the Opera House, the Veterans' War Memorial, Temple Emanuel (Arthur Lansburgh, Associate Architect) and the Federal Office Buildings were being done. If I stopped in the morning with Tim at one of his jobs, this too was permitted.

The four plus years I was with Bakewell & Brown were very good. It must have been about midway in those years, say 1927, that Arthur Brown and John Bakewell agreed to dissolve their partnership. This was very difficult for all the men in the office, for both Bakewell with his great kindliness, and Brown with his unquestioned genius were loved and admired by all and the choice as to whom one would "go with" was traumatic. Ernest Weihe became John Bakewell's partner. The others, particularly Ed Frick and Larry Kruse, stayed with Arthur Brown. (Later, upon the retirement of both Bakewell and Brown, Weihe, Frick and Kruse regrouped, formed their firm and were very successful.)

I went with "Uncle John" and Weihe. Ernest Weihe was my favorite patron and he afforded me opportunities in work which were exceptional. Years later when I applied for the state architectural license he wrote the Board, saying something like "...and even if Milt has been working in his brother Tim's office for 6 or 7 years now, I'm certain he has not fallen to the point where he could have forgotten his good early training!" No wonder I think of him with love and thankfulness.

That office, Bakewell & Brown, on the top (eighth) floor of 251 Kearny Street, I shall never forget. The men in the office had fun, lots of it, and I had my good share of it. With all except Brown, Bakewell, Weihe and Frick in the one undivided "drafting room," rubber band shooting, eraser throwing and dice shaking were not that unusual, not however when Uncle John or Mr. Brown were likely to appear!

It was in this period that the San Francisco Stock Exchange Competition took place. Six San Francisco firms were chosen to compete: Bakewell & Brown, Bliss & Faville, Lewis Hobart, George Kelham, Weeks & Day, and my brother (e.g., Miller & Pflueger). There, where I was working, I saw the classic design develop, all the while knowing that from my brother's office would come a modern concept. When my brother's design was declared the winner, even I received congratulations from the fellows in "my" office; after all, they too had won competitions such as our majestic San Francisco City Hall, the undoubted masterpiece of Classicism in our country.

The Stock Exchange competition building was not built; the Stock Exchange in lieu bought the U.S. Sub-Treasury building at the corner of Pine and Sansome Streets. Tim remodeled the Treasury into the Trading Room and a new 12-story office building was connected thereto.

I must note that in the very early 1920s, Tim had designed the new San Francisco Stock Exchange building on Bush Street in the strict classic tradition, with columns and pediments, a la Metropolitan Life. These examples were evidence of his versatility, but his atelier work in his early years presaged what was to come when opportunity presented itself.

The new projects in Tim's office led to my asking if I could enter his office. He consented; and in 1929 my real association with Tim's work began, at 580 Market Street where we have had our offices for nearly 60 years.

23. PARAMOUNT THEATER, Oakland, 1931 (Rob Super). The auditorium ceiling, constructed of bright metal vertical fins in a lacelike pattern, is suspended from the reflecting ceiling of the light chamber above. The changing chromatic colors of all hues controlled by circuitry, switches and dimmers, filter through and reflect from the sides of the vertical fins. The sensation is as the light of day from dawn to sunset and the fins become clouds of lace.

THE PARAMOUNT THEATER & THE STOCK EXCHANGE

When I entered the office, the most exciting projects in the design stage were the Stock Exchange and the Paramount Theater; others, such as the El Rey Theater, the Bal Tabarin and the Pine Street addition to the Metropolitan Life were also being worked upon. It was a very busy office, and many talented men were here at the time; Nathan Larson, Gerald Fitzgerald, Michael Goodman, Al Jaehne, Harry Leason, Ted Bernardi, Clarence Mayhew, to name those who readily come to mind. I'm sure with diligent search, we could find "time cards," but this is not a history and those unmentioned are also thought of with great warmth and thankfulness.

Those of us who actually worked on the Paramount Theater really enjoyed it; so full of decoration, new and innovative in every detail. If a few, now in retrospect, wish to think of it as pretentious, even gaudy, let them. Remember, this was in the time of Fanchon and Marco, dancing girls, Rube Wolf, extravaganza, fun, the Roaring '20s. To merely term it a classic of the Art Deco period is an understatement.

Certainly, our library had fine architectural books and magazines; those illustrating the Paris Exposition of 1925, for instance, were sources of decorative inspiration. But most were "new" and completely original. The metal "fin" ceilings (also employed in the Stock Exchange

24. PARAMOUNT THEATER, 1931, (Gabriel Moulin). Theater Auditorium. A bold profusion of adornment, creating a world of make-believe.

25. PARAMOUNT THEATER, (Gabriel Moulin). Exterior view. The facade Puppeteers, in color-glaze tile.

26. PARAMOUNT THEATER, 1931 (Gabriel Moulin). The Grand Lobby—light and color. Metal fins are again used as in the auditorium.

27. PARAMOUNT THEATER, (Rob Super). Sculptured wall detail.

28. SAN FRANCISCO STOCK EXCHANGE, San Francisco, 1930 (Gabriel Moulin). The Trading Room. Metal Fins, a trade mark of the office, (and patented) are used in the ceiling, filtering daylight from a skylight above.

Trading Room and the Bal Tabarin) were completely original in concept; in fact, Tim was coerced into obtaining a patent on the principle. The indirect lighting in the plenum above the fins provided all color ranges and hues. The decorative walls of the theater, cast in plaster from models sculpted by Robert Howard and covered with silver-gold leaf, were drawn in the most careful detail by Gerald Fitzgerald in our office; this was true also of the proscenium arch, the organ grilles, and all ornamentation, even to lighting fixtures, which were designed in our office.

The glazed tile puppeteers of the facade were also drawn and colored by "Fitz" Fitzgerald. Small scale black and white sections were projected to full size on billboard paper at Foster and Kleiser. At full size, we drew the projected lines on the paper and from these drawings Gladding-McBean, in Lincoln, CA, manufactured the individual tiles. We had great fun. It was that kind of an office, with something new and exciting all the time.

The theater is now the home of the Oakland Symphony and Performing Arts, having been restored and refinished in every detail to its original state; and in 1976, it was designated as a National Historic Landmark and placed on the National Register of Historic Places.

And what of the San Francisco Stock Exchange with its magnificent Trading Room, and the renowned Lunch Club on the top two floors of the connecting building? On this project, Tim brought into full play the work of artists. The heroic Ralph Stackpole pylon sculptures—how did Tim persuade the client to spend $50,000 there; and to bring Diego Rivera to do his great stair hall fresco in the Lunch Club; to integrate the talent and work of all the other artists such as Bob Howard and Adeline Kent (Bob's wife), Ruth Cravath, Otis Oldfield, Jacques Schneir and others? Only a dynamic nature and persuasive sureness of his own convictions could bring this about.

There was a slight rest in the early part of the Depression, when for a year or so there were only a few in the office and when jobs such as the George Washington High School, the Alhambra Theater, a prototype Standard Oil Station, and others kept us busy; the Circus Room in the Fairmont Hotel, with the Bruton sisters' murals, was also in the early 1930s.

29. SAN FRANCISCO STOCK EXCHANGE, 1930. (rendering: Michael Goodman).

30. SAN FRANCISCO STOCK EXCHANGE, (Gabriel Moulin). Exterior view. The remodeled U.S. Sub Treasury Building and the new Office Building.

31. SAN FRANCISCO STOCK EXCHANGE COMPETITION, San Francisco, 1929 (rendering: Hugh Ferriss). Nathan Larson of the office staff made the submission rendering of the award winning design for a new San Francisco Stock Exchange building. After the award, Hugh Ferriss was commissioned to do a rendering; this is his inspirational drawing.

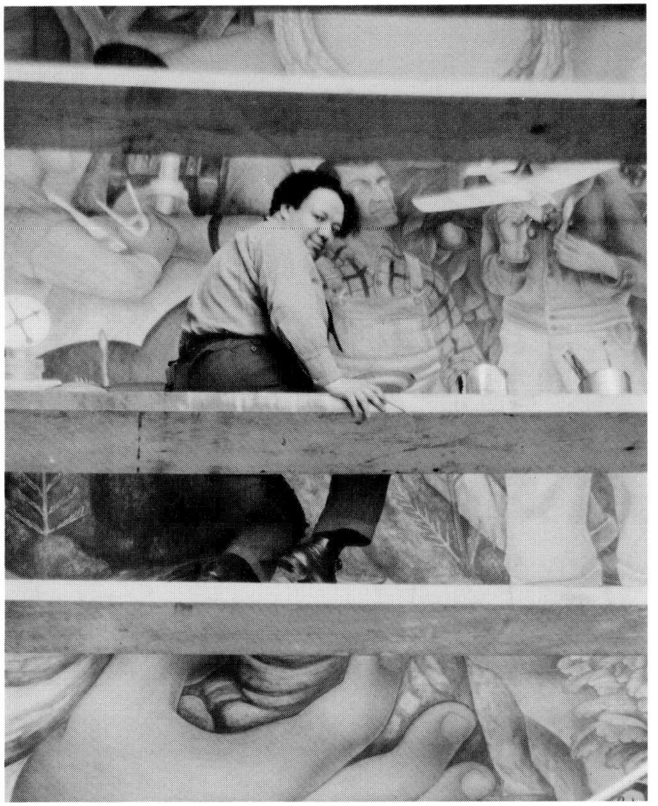

32. SAN FRANCISCO STOCK EXCHANGE, 1930 (Peter A. Juley & Son). Rivera at work on the fresco.

33. SAN FRANCISCO STOCK EXCHANGE, 1930 (Gabriel Moulin). The Sansome Street Entrance Lobby of the office building which adjoins the sub-treasury at the corner of Pine and Sansome Streets. A "paper-fold" gold leafed ceiling, with polished black marble walls.

34. SAN FRANCISCO STOCK EXCHANGE, (Peter A. Juley & Son). The Diego Rivera fresco in the stair hall of the quarters for the Stock Exchange Lunch Club. Helen Wills Moody, the classic beauty of tennis fame, was Rivera's model for the featured portrait. Before her stands young Peter Stackpole, with his model airplane. Subsequent to the Stock Exchange Competition, it was determined in lieu thereof to purchase the U.S. Sub Treasury, remodel it, and add thereto a new office building.

35. SAN FRANCISCO-OAKLAND BAY BRIDGE, 1937 (rendering: Carl Nuess, photograph: Gabriel Moulin). Rendering of San Francisco approach and anchorage. Without embellishment, the basic engineering was detailed and characterized as such. There is no need for "architectural treatment."

36. SAN FRANCISCO-OAKLAND BAY BRIDGE, 1937 (Gabriel Moulin). Twin spans with central anchorage.

THE SAN FRANCISCO-OAKLAND BAY BRIDGE

Then came the call that Governor James Rolph had appointed a three-man Consulting Board of Architects to the engineering team already working on the San Francisco—Oakland Bay Bridge; Tim the Chairman, with Arthur Brown, Jr. and John Donovan of Oakland. The engineers had an architectural concept and were well along with the basic engineering. Charles Purcell was the Chief Engineer and he had assembled a team of outstanding engineering consultants. The architectural "treatment," for such it could be termed, was neo-Gothic or Classic as the case might be. Tim's ideas prevailed and the stylistic embellishment was eliminated. The towers, anchorages, piers, tunnel became truly stripped to the basics. This was not easily accomplished.

However, Tim's perceptiveness prevailed; the realization that good engineering, well proportioned and well detailed, was also good architecture, was accepted. This was all accomplished in our office. Sid Gorman, the engineers' representative, became a part of the office, conveying the constraints and parameters within which we could work. The design of the Terminal and approaches became part of the Architects' task. The "hands-off" direction which saddened the office most was the engineering east of Yerba Buena; this was too far along, and redesign was not to be permitted.

Let one not believe that the design of the Bay Bridge just happened as a result of the elimination of cosmetic treatment. This was the first step. Proportion, scale and character—the elements which, if right, produce good engineering and good architecture (they are one and the same)—were studied to the greatest degree possible, given the mandates.

Think of it—the two great bridges, the Golden Gate and the Bay, being built at the same time, in the decade of the Depression and the start of World War. Irving Morrow, Consulting Architect to Joseph Strauss the dreamer-engineer of the "impossible to build" Golden Gate Bridge, did a most magnificent job, and of the two bridges it has endeared itself to most. With its tremendous single span dictating the high towers, the inherent proportions are inspiring, beautiful to behold.

Such is not the advantage of the Bay Bridge. With shorter double spans and a central anchorage, the given proportions are less inspiring and the solution totally different. The Bay towers, with almost equal height above and below the suspended roadway trusses, are designed as one element, with cross bracing from water line to tower top. The Gate towers, with almost a three to one ratio (above roadway and below respectively) have cross bracing below and "portal" or horizontal bracing above.

Different requisites produce different solutions. One could thus analyze and dwell upon the design processes which created these two magnificent bridges.

Charles Purcell and his consultant engineers, Glen Woodruff and Charles Andrews were two with whom we worked very closely. Engineers were the prime force, but when ability and mutual respect prevail there is not conflict. Purcell became a life-long friend and years later was instrumental in my doing the Headquarters for the Motor Vehicle Department in Sacramento.

It is almost unconscionable to write of the Bay Bridge with such brevity. The work was fascinating, and the good fortune to play such an important role in its fruition was a source of great pride and satisfaction to Tim and the office. It is well that the story of both bridges was so copiously documented. This helps in the alleviation of my shortcomings.

37. *THE GOLDEN GATE INTERNATIONAL EXPOSITION, Treasure Island, San Francisco, 1939-1940 (Gabriel Moulin). Overview of model with Arthur Brown, Jr.'s Tower at focal point, the intersection of main north-south and east-west axis.*

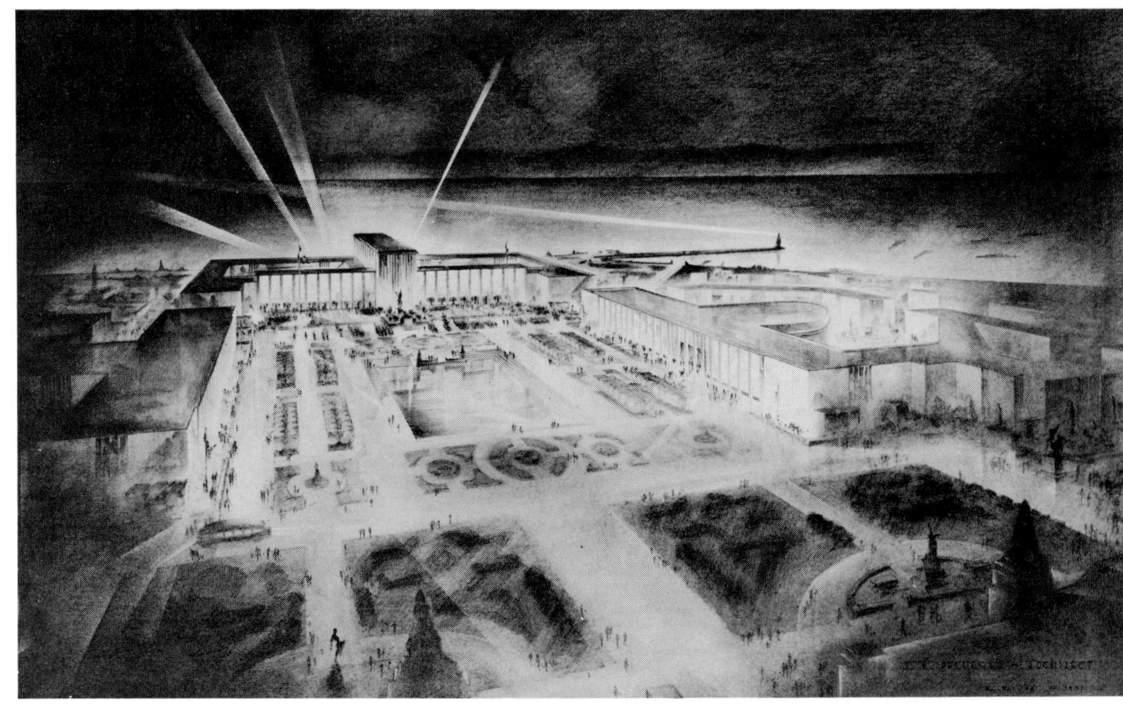

38. *THE GOLDEN GATE INTERNATIONAL EXPOSITION, (Gabriel Moulin). Rendering of Esplanade; Lagoon in forefront of Federal Building.*

THE GOLDEN GATE INTERNATIONAL EXPOSITION

The design of the Golden Gate Exposition began at the same time as the bridge. Tim was on the Board of Architects. The other members were George Kelham, Arthur Brown, Jr., William G. Merchant, Lewis Hobart and Ernest Weihe. Edward Frick was in general charge of the Exposition's architectural office. Each member of the Board, in addition to his personal involvement, assigned his representative-designer to the Architect-Engineer Exposition office.

After establishing the overall plan, each member of the Board was responsible for a specific part of the master plan. The Court of the Pacific was Tim's, and here again the artists' collaboration was brought into full play. Ralph Stackpole's heroic Pacifica against a "prayer curtain" of shimmering white metal, the Bruton sisters' great mural, and the fountain with its sculptures of the people of the Pacific were features of the Court. Tim either could not or did not dissuade his good friend, Ralph, from folding

39. THE GOLDEN GATE INTERNATIONAL EXPOSITION, 1939-1940 (Gabriel Moulin). Court of Pacifica. A sparkling metal "prayer curtain" is the background for Ralph Stackpole's "Pacifica." The "Peoples of the Pacific" fountain is in the foreground.

the drapery of Pacifica into the monogram TLP!

In addition to his work as a member of the Architectural Board, Tim was also the Executive Architect for the State of California Commission for the Exposition. Here, in our offices we did the Federal Building. He was the Architect for the Palace of Fine Arts, which was housed in one of the permanent structures (for the future airport, an ill-conceived proposal and fortunately discarded). He was the General Director for the Exhibition of Fine Arts.

Though the New York World's Fair of 1939 expressed the world of tomorrow, it was the Federal Building on Treasure Island that was described in the foremost architectural magazine as the "most imaginative of modern architectural ventures" of either fair. The Federal Building was not only imaginative, it was designed with an awareness and discernment found very rarely. TIME Magazine, in its January 2, 1939 issue, had an article about the Exposition which was shortly to open. The entire article, not too lengthy, had this to say:

"PACIFIC PAGEANT

The two biggest shows in the land of the free this year will be at Flushing, L.I., and on San Francisco Bay. To state them, businessmen have dug down for millions of dollars, politicians have played their cards, engineers have sweated, architects have dreamed, press agents have run wild, artists have cried aloud. Located smack in the center of the two greatest metropolitan areas in the United States, each will choke its already surfeited neighborhood with million and millions of citizens out for a good time. To each will come travellers seeking knowledge of the world and its wonders. So runs the half-meretricious, half-genuine promise of World's Fairs.

In the East this converging flood of populations is still four months away, but San Francisco has only six weeks before the great visitation begins. The FORTUNE Survey for November deduced that 24.3%, or 31,590,000 of the nation's 130,000,000 people expect to go to New York, 6.9% or 8,970,000 to San Francisco.

Last week, curious critical San Franciscans took a last look around their Exposition's 'Treasure Island', probably about to be closed to visitors while 3,000 workmen go on double shift to polish it off for opening day.

40. THE GOLDEN GATE INTERNATIONAL EXPOSITION, 1939-1940 (Gabriel Moulin). The Federal Building. It features the colonnade of our United States, 48 timbered columns open to the sky. Muralled walls enclose courts which open to the colonnade.

Ocean City. The reclaimers of Flushing dump could be reasonably sure that any exposition erected there would be a delightful improvement on the scene, but San Francisco's exposition builders were far from such a certainty. For the city and harbor of San Francisco constitute one of the great urban beauties of North America. San Francisco Bay is not only vast—48 miles long, embracing 450 square miles of roadstead—but magnificently visible, cupped by the steeply carved mountains of the coast range. San Francisco rises in clean, pale tiers of buildings on the hilly peninsula between this shining water and the Pacific Ocean.

The site chosen for the 'Golden Gate International Exposition' placed it in isolated contrast to these surroundings, had a decisive influence on its builders. San Francisco needed an airport before it needed a Fair, and the best place for an airport was determined as early as 1931 by the Junior Chamber of Commerce. Credit for putting two and two together is given to Air-enthusiast Henry Eickhoff Jr., who began thumping in 1933 for an exposition along with the airport, on the ground that each would help build the other. Three years more and a fleet of dredges appeared off the wooded hump of Yerba Buena Island between San Francisco and Oakland and began pumping black sand from the Bay bottom, slopping it over Yerba Buena shoals. With the help of Army engineers, WPA labor and a grant of $6,250,000 from the Federal Government, a mile-long island was sucked from the Bay to serve as San Francisco's fairground in 1939 and its airport forever after.

Pleasuredom. Local precedent for the Fair builders was San Francisco's Panama-Pacific International Exposition of 1915, a glittering tour de force by the smartest Beaux Arts architects of the day. Held to celebrate the opening of the Panama Canal, it appropriately linked East Coast and West Coast on its board of architects. Tenderly remembered in San Francisco, the Panama-Pacific Exposition had no influence for the good on United States architecture.

For San Francisco's present exposition, subtitled 'A Pageant of the Pacific', the board of architects was an all-Western team. Chairman was George William Kelham, who had also been chief architect for the 1915 show. When he died two years ago he was succeeded by Arthur Brown, Jr., another Panama-Pacific architect. Outstanding characteristic of the rest of the Fair architects, as of the exposition they designed, was their collaborative harmony. Fellow members of the Bohemian Club, august sanctuary of San Francisco tradition, most of them shared a mellow view of architecture and were damned if they would kill themselves advancing the modern cause in new materials and organic form. New York City's 1939 Fair already had a lien on the World of Tomorrow. Chairman Kelham and crew therefore plumped for a pleasuredom on 'Treasure Island', an imaginative, quasi-Oriental 'Never-Never-Land'.

Conceivably, nothing could have been worse. Fortunately, the Fair architects had taste in using their natural site. By laying out their timber and plaster buildings as a windowless 'walled city', completely enclosing an L-shaped set of avenues and courts, they made a sheer 80-foot bulwark a quarter of a mile long against the trade wind that blows off the Pacific. To keep the wind out at the west entrances, blue-eyed, sandy-haired Architect Ernest Weihe, fussing around with an electric fan, feathers and a cardboard model, devised 'wind baffles'—a series of 80-foot vertical slabs placed like converging flys on a stage, with open passages to left and right between them. The clean monumentality of this effect was also used to set off Sculptor Ralph Stackpole's heroic-sized statue, Pacifica.

Basically nothing but enormous sheds, the main exposition buildings, stuccoed in 'warm ivory' and unobtrusive pastel shades, owe much of their exoticism to 'elephant towers', whose angles of light and shadow are softened by the Bay's hazy atmosphere. Mercifully softened also is the 400-bell carillon. Last week San Francisco critics bore down hard on the Tower. Said Sculptor Beniamino Bufano: 'It should have been a mosque or a minaret.' Said Sculptor Ralph Stackpole: 'The thing is up. What can you do about it?'

Modern Colonnade. Restrained as its glamor mostly is, and unified by a compact and accessible plan, the Fair may well weary its visitors less, refresh them more than if it had serious pretensions. From a structural standpoint it is preeminently stage design, fakery. Two big hangar buildings of steel and concrete and an administration building, all permanent fixtures of the new airports, are exceptions to this rule, and greatest exception of all is the Federal Building, separated from the rest by a lagoon and a parade ground. This is the work of San Francisco's genial, hard-bitten, unpredictable Timothy Ludwig Pflueger.

A self-made architect who got his schooling in offices, Timothy Pflueger is all for 'Pacific Architecture' as a reality, believes 'it's too damned bad we didn't have the Oriental influences on the coast instead of the European.' As President of the San Francisco Art Association, he staged, from 1934 to 1937, the hugest, most exotic super-deMille costume balls in San Francisco's history. For the Federal Building, however, he produced a fine, occidental job of economy, stateliness and rational planning.

At its centre in an open court, a colonnade of 48 timberwork columns, four abreast and twelve in a row, rises 100 feet to symbolize the States of the Union. At once simple, honest, impressive and cheap, this stunt utilizes the sky and water of the Bay. On each side of the columns Architect Pflueger designed other open courts, surrounded by a light and trimly built structure of four-by-eight-foot plywood panels, a strong beautiful surface, more native than stucco to forested California. About 20 nations of the Pacific, from Peru to Japan, are building more or less authentic pavilions along the Pacific Lagoon. None is a saner expression of national character than Pflueger's for the U.S.A."

During the Exposition, we would often go to the Top of the Mark, which had been completed just in time for the Exposition opening. Here, from "our room," Tim, with good reason, would look with pleasure and pride over his city to the sparkling lights of the Bay Bridge leading to the brilliantly illuminated Treasure Island.

How can I leave the Exposition, without reference to two of Tim's close friends, without whom it could never have been realized: Leland Cutler, one of San Francisco's most prominent and distinguished civic leaders, the President of the Exposition, and George Creel, the Federal Commissioner for the Exposition, the man who had an open door to the office of President Franklin Roosevelt, an ardent supporter.

While so reminiscing, the Bay Bridge, as well as the Exposition, was in very great part due to Leland Cutler, Florence McAuliffe, Lloyd Dinkelspiel, Governor James Rolph, Mayor Angelo Rossi and many other close friends. All of this has been clearly documented and the record is there for those who want to know of unselfish, devoted dedication. These men I wish never to forget, and through the intercedence of Tim, I had the rare privilege of participation and in many instances the beginning of friendship with men I greatly admired.

THE LATE 1930s AND EARLY 1940s

The exciting projects already mentioned by no means represented all the work of those years in the office. The San Francisco Junior College work started in 1937 with the first Master Plan and the first Academic Building. The development of the entire Main Campus of the Junior College, or the San Francisco Community College as it is now named, is but one example of the continuity of which we are proud. Work for I. Magnin began in 1937 with the interiors of the main Los Angeles Wilshire store. The Abraham Lincoln High School followed, as did the Circus Room in the Fairmont in 1934 and the Top of the Mark, which was completed in 1939 and which rightfully gained its world fame. Clubs, restaurants and lounges were exciting planning and design problems, bringing forth new concepts in accord with particular requirements.

At the Top of the Mark, the design problem was met directly, with exterior walls being removed to as great a degree as structurally feasible to permit the widest expanse of panoramic views. The room itself was subrogated entirely to the limitless space beyond, and in every form, shape and detail, the room became not a room but a

41. TOP OF THE MARK, MARK HOPKINS HOTEL, San Francisco, 1939 (Ansel Adams). Subliminal Architecture. The view is the thing.

42. TOP OF THE MARK, MARK HOPKINS HOTEL, 1939 (Ansel Adams). The Central Bar, surrounded by window seating.

43. PATENT LEATHER LOUNGE, ST. FRANCIS HOTEL, San Francisco, 1939 (Ansel Adams). Decorative lighting with new material.

44. PATENT LEATHER LOUNGE, ST. FRANCIS HOTEL, 1939 (Ansel Adams). Dorothy Wright Liebes' window drapes.

45. PATENT LEATHER LOUNGE, ST. FRANCIS HOTEL, (Ansel Adams). A room of opulence.

part of the space beyond. Just the reverse was true in the Patent Leather Lounge or Orchid Room at the St. Francis Hotel where the interest was in the room; a molded translucent ceiling of Lucite, then in its earliest development phase, was dominant with its ever changing back lighting, as were Dorothy Liebes' grand window drapes (yet another of Tim's closest friends). Nor should I forget Ansel Adams, the great photographer, persuaded by Tim and because of friendship took photos of these rooms, a task which Ansel very rarely undertook, but one which of course resulted in architectural photography as grand as his natural photography.

Another "first" of these years was the Union Square Garage and Plaza, first conceived in the mid '30s, opened in 1942, a project which Tim was called upon to describe in cities all over our country since it was the first of its kind, an underground garage beneath a City park, built without City money (the entire project becoming City-owned within 20 years).

Here the concept evolved that the true park must be preserved. Low, two feet high planter walls on all four boundary sidewalks afford spatial relationships and vistas into the green. With change in street grades of twenty-five feet, this was a challenge in planning and landscaping, relating structure, planning and circulation,

46. UNION SQUARE PLAZA AND GARAGE, San Francisco, 1942 (Gabriel Moulin). Plaza looking northwest. 450 Sutter upper right. What can be difficult in designing a park surface over a subsurface garage? Surely this poses no problems? That would be the reaction of the casual, unsuspecting observer. The near street corner, in this photo, (Geary and Stockton) is 25 feet lower than the diagonal opposite corner (Post and Powell), a given condition. A second condition, self-imposed in this case, is that sidewalk boundaries around the Square be low–seat-high walls, preserving openness to and from the Square on all sides. The two conditions are counteracting and the solution much more subtle than apparent. Add the condition of good garage planning beneath a roof which slopes in all directions and one finds that, indeed, the solution is complex. If in the end, it all seems quite natural and fitting, that is good architecture.

47. CIRCUS LOUNGE, FAIRMONT HOTEL, San Francisco, 1934 (Gabriel Moulin). The Bruton circus murals with gold leaf backgrounds are dominant.

and excavation to depths of over fifty feet. Ingress, egress and internal circulation was so forward thinking and well planned, that in 1961 it was possible for us to convert from attendant operation to an equally efficient self-parking operation without external change of any kind.

Upon Tim's death in 1946, the Board of Directors of the Union Square Garage Corporation wrote a testament in his memory. It need only be quoted to indicate the regard in which he was held.

TIMOTHY L. PFLUEGER
1892-1946

The directors of the Union Square Garage Corporation record with profound sorrow the untimely passing of its architect and director, Timothy L. Pflueger, in whose going San Francisco has lost a distinguished citizen, and the world a great artist. In his illustrious, although comparatively short career, he did much to clothe in lasting beauty the city that he loved. San Francisco will long remember Timothy L. Pflueger, not only for his creative genius, but above and beyond that for his steadfast refusal to compromise his ideals. In his standards, mediocrity was unknown. We whose privilege it was to be his associates in the re-creation of Union Square, where he wrought incredible beauty in the surface restoration while accomplishing the miraculous in carrying out the functional objectives of the project, shall always cherish in our memories the high ideals and sound principals with which he imbued all with whom he came in contact. To his family we extend our deep-felt sympathy at their loss, which, we pray, is mitigated to some extent by their pride in the glory of his achievements and in the universal esteem in which he was held. This testament in memoriam has been entered in our minutes in the form of resolutions, and it was ordered that an engraved copy hereof shall be presented to the family of Timothy L. Pflueger.

F. M. McAuliffe
Secretary

Carlton H. Wall
President

48. BAL TABARIN, San Francisco, 1933 (Ansel Adams). A ceiling and stage backdrop of indirect light, reflections from curved bright metal strips.

49. THE OLYMPIC CLUB, San Francisco, 1955 (Joshua Freiwald). The back bar at the City Club features drawings of Howard Brodie.

50. ROOSEVELT JUNIOR HIGH SCHOOL, San Francisco, 1924 (Gabriel Moulin). Patterns — the ornamental development, using the typical units of brick masonry.

51. GEORGE WASHINGTON HIGH SCHOOL, San Francisco, 1932 (J. Thomas Pflueger). The portico entrance to the Auditorium with the cast-in-place concrete frieze in the forefront.

52. *I. MAGNIN AND COMPANY, San Francisco, 1947 (Gabriel Moulin). Clothed in Vermont marble, with un-mullioned plate glass windows framed in stainless steel, it says, 'Within these walls, only the finest.'*

I. MAGNIN & COMPANY

Much was written of Tim's work. Projects received acclaim and his total commitment and creativity was recognized. Who am I to recall or add thereto, particularly without research, study and available references. It is done as a very personal expression of thankfulness and appreciation. A heritage such as this comes to few men, and I am reminded of this each day as I glance at the testimony of the Union Square Garage directors which hangs over my desk.

To skip so quickly over accomplishments such as Tim's despairs me. I was too near then, and his end which came so few years after completion of Union Square and in the midst of ever greater accomplishment, causes me even now to be brief and hold much within.

We were very busy in the 1940s and several of the most memorable projects will not be so lightly dismissed.

I have spoken of Tim's work for I. Magnin & Co, Grover Magnin to be specific, for he and Tim were Owner/Architect, respectively and period. They traveled in Europe together, searched and found art, and commissioned artists who worked particulary in glass. These works were incorporated in the interiors of the stores, Wilshire Avenue in Los Angeles in the 1930s, where Tim did the interiors and again in the later stores. At the time of Tim's death, our I. Magnin stores were being built in Santa Barbara and Beverly Hills, and in the office we were still working on the Geary and Stockton Store in San Francisco. To me, the latter will always be in the top drawer, a building of "timeless beauty," and these words are not mine but those of a contemporary nationally known architect.

This was originally the Butler Bulding, an office building for doctors and dentists. Structural investigation indicated the steel frame could be strengthened to meet the code and most of the reinforced floor slabs met requirements, but that was it. All else was demolished and because of internal planning many columns were removed or relocated. So we very literally started from scratch.

53. I. MAGNIN AND COMPANY, 1947 (Charles H. Hays). Main Entrance.

54. I. MAGNIN AND COMPANY, (Charles H. Hays). Interior. Elegant uncluttered space.

55. *UNION SQUARE PLAZA AND GARAGE-1942, I. MAGNIN & CO.-1947, (Roger Sturtevant). Looking Southeast across the Plaza. The rebuilt Dewey Monument and I. Magnin & Co. The dismantled, rebuilt monument was made earthquake resistant by coring the solid granite column sections, filling same with heavily reinforced concrete, creating a continuous new column from foundation of garage to top of monument.*

WHEN TIME STOPPED

There were other significant projects in the office at this time, primarily the Herbert C. Moffitt Teaching Hospital and the Richmond Civic Center.

The former had been in the office on and off since the '30s. Funding and the big question of just what role the University of California Medical Center was to play delayed the project for many years, but in 1946 we were in the preliminary design stage of the 550 bed hosptial.

The Richmond Civic Center was now in its early conceptual stage. A Master Plan and the general components were established. Sketches suitable for promotion and public interest had been made but the bonds were still to be sold. Wayne E. Thompson, then the City Manager of Richmond, was a driving force in the ultimate accomplishment of the War Memorial Center.

Quiet, unassuming, with great knowledge and foresight, he with Tim formed the perfect combination to initiate and foresee the first modern unified Civic Center in our country. The City had grown tremendously in the war years and was ready for leadership in such an undertaking.

The I. Magnin stores in Santa Barbara and Beverly Hills were in construction; the San Francisco store was nearing the construction phase. We were starting to program additions to Mt. Zion Hospital here in the City and Mills Hospital in San Mateo.

This then, was the status of our office when on the evening of November 18, 1946, after leaving the Olympic Club, Tim suffered a heart attack on Post Street and was gone.

Just a year before, on November 23, 1945, Howard Meyers, the publisher of the Architectural Forum, hosted a luncheon at the Manhattan Club in New York City honoring Timothy Pflueger. Tim was honored in absentia, having been suddenly detained in San Francisco.

However, there were present Alvar Aalto, Hugh Ferris, Edward D. Stone, Philip Johnson, Henry Wright, George Howe, Wallace Harrison and Frank Lloyd Wright, a representation of the finest, and friends, all. Howard Meyers, in whom I too had a friend because of Tim, had for a number of years wanted to publish a special issue on Tim's work. I know it was not done because Tim felt there would be time for that in the future.

On that evening in 1946 when I received the phone call, having just said "so long" a few hours earlier, time stopped.

12
1939

THANK YOU, TIM

It is difficult for me to write of Tim personally, Tim the man. I know I took too much of his life for granted.

So many were touched by his love, kindness and generous nature. Throughout his life, and after, I learned from friends and acquaintances, never from Tim, of one kind deed and then another. If he alone could not take care of the entire matter, he would touch a friend quietly and quickly, for he too was so often called upon, friend upon friend, as it should be and was.

In the years still to be given me, never need I be reminded of his love, thoughtfulness and unstinting help to his family. All shared fully and constantly in the rewards of his success. My own share transcends all. No one could receive more.

A life, a career, comparatively short but filled with wondrous things, had suddenly been taken. What were my thoughts, if indeed I had any, on that evening of November 18, 1946? If time did not stop, it was surely one of those uncertain beats of time, and the path ahead seemed in darkness.

Stronger hands held mine. The passing days were to bring thoughts of the years of love and indoctrination. Amidst grief, the night turned to day, our resolve was there.

NIGHT OF APPRECIATION · 1939
WHEN THE
WEIGHT OF
GLORY FALLS
UPON A MAN

TO THE STAFF IN APPRECIATION

When I returned to the office the well of sympathy was full. My few words to the staff were that with their help and understanding, and with the spirit of Tim around us, continuity was certain. I say, and it has always been so, that the loyalty and talent of the staff is unmatched.

Many times in the history of our office there were temptations to branch out, to "go big." Whether or not we were right, this was not our desire. I know that Tim was asked many times why the firm did not take this course and I have been also. San Francisco has been our home and we would keep it so. A good medium size office, one perfectly capable of doing the big projects, has been our choice.

Certainly in a long history, personnel changes for the usual reasons, but an experienced team of professionals, vital and innovative, coupled with the infusion of younger men who grow up in the firm, all made possible by continuity of work, has been a policy which we believe produces the best results in the full range of an ever more complex profession. To name past and present individuals who have and are contributing so directly would be a subject in itself, one which I would love to address in the greatest detail. That will not be done. However I cannot go on without paying tribute to certain associates, those who in my time have particularly contributed in a very personal endeavor to our continuity.

Leffler B. Miller came into our office in 1939, directly after having worked for Lewis P. Hobart in the 1939-40 San Francisco World's Fair Architects' office. Prior to that he had worked for Willis Polk, the Allied Architects Office in Los Angeles and the State Office in Sacramento. In his distinguished association in our office, his contributions have influenced the character and integrity of the office. Since 1971 his participation has been on a part-time basis. He is a remarkable, talented, gentle man, a beloved friend.

William A. Hutcheson, Jr., U.S. Naval Academy graduate 1945, came into our office in 1947 after his navy service without formal architectural training. His activity as designer, production director and project architect has been invaluable to the reputation of the firm. He represents the qualities we are most proud of, and he is inspiring to the young members of our firm.

Carl H. Riesen was one of our bright stars. Entering the office in 1946, he was with us without interruption until his untimely death in 1970 at the age of 54. Extremely talented, a very close friend, he contributed immeasurably to our success.

Joseph Scoma came to us in 1929, also my first year in Tim's office, and he was with us until his retirement in 1972.

Edward Hicks, until his retirement in 1971, had been with us for well over twenty years.

Margretha Budd was Tim's secretary and then mine for an unbroken period of 37 years until she retired in 1968. She entered the office, she still maintains, on a "temporary" basis. Joyce Norman, our administrative secretary without whom we could hardly function, has been with us more than twenty years. We bring staff like this to tears at times, but perhaps we are doing something right.

Lee R. Greenfield, after some years of private practice in Texas and further experience in military and public works, entered our office in 1957 and very quickly assumed responsibilities as a project coordinator.

People of the past and present, imprinted in my mind, whose names must be set down lest I forget: Sco De Long, Byron Lundberg, Bob Colby, Frank Krueger, Jim Tuley, Rafe Keegan, Jack Sagen, Marina van Overbeek, James Davis.

To all who have been or are now in our office we say thanks for devotion, loyalty and extraordinary talent.

56. CIVIC CENTER, Richmond, 1949-51 (Phil Fein). City Hall, plaza facade.

57. CIVIC CENTER, Richmond, 1949-51 (Phil Fein). Plaza, with Auditorium—City Hall—Public Safety. The first unified Civic Center in our country where the City Hall, Public Safety, Memorial Auditorium and Public Library buildings were planned and built as one cohesive complex.

THE 1950s AND 1960s: CIVIC CENTERS

As said earlier, I received my State License in 1939. In those days, and I think it is still so, without a college degree one must have had at least 12 years of office experience before being allowed to take the State Board. I became Tim's chief aide and his partner. He had a partnership agreement drawn, but we never got around to signing it. We really saw no need of it. Lacking such, however, made it necessary for me as an individual to enter into new agreements with our clients after Tim's death; and while this presented no real problems, the details were time consuming.

The bonds for the Richmond Civic Center were sold and the Center was constructed in phases. The City Hall and Public Safety Buildings were completed in 1949, the Library in 1950 and the Auditorium and Arts Center in 1951. The phasing was required for operational continuity, demolition of existing structures, closing of streets and related conditions. Its "fast-tracking," however, was economically sound; even then inflation existed though not in its present state.

It is interesting to note that the entire Center was constructed at a building construction cost

58. CIVIC CENTER-CITY HALL, Sunnyvale, 1958 (Joshua Freiwald). A park-like informal center.

of approximately $4,250,000. Today its cost would far exceed $30,000,000. The Memorial Civic Center is the cultural center of the City not only by virtue of the inclusion of an Arts Center, but also because its Auditorium provides features which make possible events of every nature from sports to conventions and performing arts. The entire Auditorium floor, levelled at stage level, can be tilted toward stage in a matter of minutes, thus providing very acceptable sight lines for stage presentations.

This Civic Center was the first "unified" center in our country, i.e., a group of buildings, similar in style and character and compatible in scale. Again I think of the pleasure it was working with Wayne Thompson, City Manager. He subsequently went to Oakland as City Manager where his outstanding accomplishments continued to draw ever increasing national attention. It came to the point where he could no longer resist private sector overtures. He accepted an executive vice-presidency with Dayton-Hudson.

From its headquarters in Minneapolis, he directs a public interest giving program which symbolizes the belief that what is good for the public is good for the corporation. Lunching with Wayne during his visits to San Francisco is always a great pleasure and most illuminating.

We are still engaged in work for the City of Richmond, and this leads me to the realization that to here the story model has been mainly chronological. To so continue would be difficult for so many of our clients have been of a constant nature.

Further involvement in civic planning and design followed the Richmond Civic Center. The Master Plan for the Sunnyvale Civic Center and the City Hall and Library, its two first units in the late '50s; the City Hall and Public Safety buildings for Modesto in the early '60s; and other projects of this nature including a prize in a Santa Rosa City Hall competition in 1965, which John and our Jim Tuley did.

59. MODESTO CITY HALL, Modesto, 1960 (Phil Fein). Sunken court below a main entrance bridge from which this photograph is taken.

THE UNIVERSITY OF SAN FRANCISCO

In the early 1940s, the UNIVERSITY OF SAN FRANCISCO embarked upon its move to become the real University of San Francisco as we now know it. At the time, there was the grand twin-spired St. Ignatius Church on the corner of Fulton Street and Parker Avenue, a hill-top landmark in our "City of Hills"; one permanent all-purpose Academic Building, now called Campion Hall; and Welch Hall, the Jesuit Fathers' Residence; the balance of the campus consisted of wartime temporary classroom structures. Before Tim's death, a Master Plan was envisioned; however, the exact nature and purposes of new facilities were not established.

After Tim's death, the Reverend Father President of the University, William J. Dunne, S.J., informed me that a funding program was well on its way and that our office was the University's Architect. The first new facility was the Richard Gleeson Library, completed in 1951, and subsequently as fund drives, major donations and continued support from the Alumni, Benefactors and Friends came forth, the University's Campus developed as its needs required.

Major buildings since Gleeson Library include James D. Phelan Hall/Student Residence in 1955 and its addition in 1961, the Memorial Gymnasium in 1959, Xavier Hall, the Jesuit Faculty Residence in 1959, the School of Law, Charles Kendrick Hall in 1962, the Charles Harney Science Center in 1964, Gillson Hall and Hayes-Healy Hall/Student Residences in 1965 and 1966, the University Center in 1966 and Cowell Hall School of Nursing in 1968.

Other University requirements have been met in existing facilities; McLaren Hall, the School of Business, a Computer Center, the activation of the former St. Ignatius High School with its Loyola Hall, the Gymnasium and Field. The names of these buildings have great significance in the history of our City and every one brings fond recollections.

This Jesuit University, first known as St. Ignatius College when it was founded in 1855 on Market Street, with several subsequent moves until its establishment on the hilltop in 1927, has truly become the University of San Francisco. Physical facilities to meet new and increasing needs are in conceptual stages constantly.

Landscaping and site development have kept pace, and very soon one ultimate goal, the elimination of all service vehicles and all parking on campus, will be accomplished. All facilities have been planned with this in mind and it will soon be a reality.

As participants in its growth, it is an honor to work with the leaders of the Jesuit community and the lay leaders of the University. I list the unbroken line of Presidents of the University with whom we have worked and are now working, those whose prayers have instilled confidence and trust and whose friendship we value so highly: William J. Dunne, S.J., John F.X. Connolly, S.J., Charles W. Dullea, S.J., Albert R. Jonsen, S.J., William C. McInness, S.J., and John J. LoSchiavo, S.J.

No, that is not enough. To not acknowledge how much these men have enriched our lives is an insensitivity for which I do not care to be responsible. We receive far more in every way than we give. Their prayers, which at times we almost accept for granted, give us life in its fullest measure.

After this was written, in 1977 the University purchased the San Francisco College for Women on Lone Mountain, just one block north of the University Campus. The beautiful college buildings and the 23-acre site—long eyed with envy by developers—adds the most significant dimension to the University which stands strong for the finest traditions of our City.

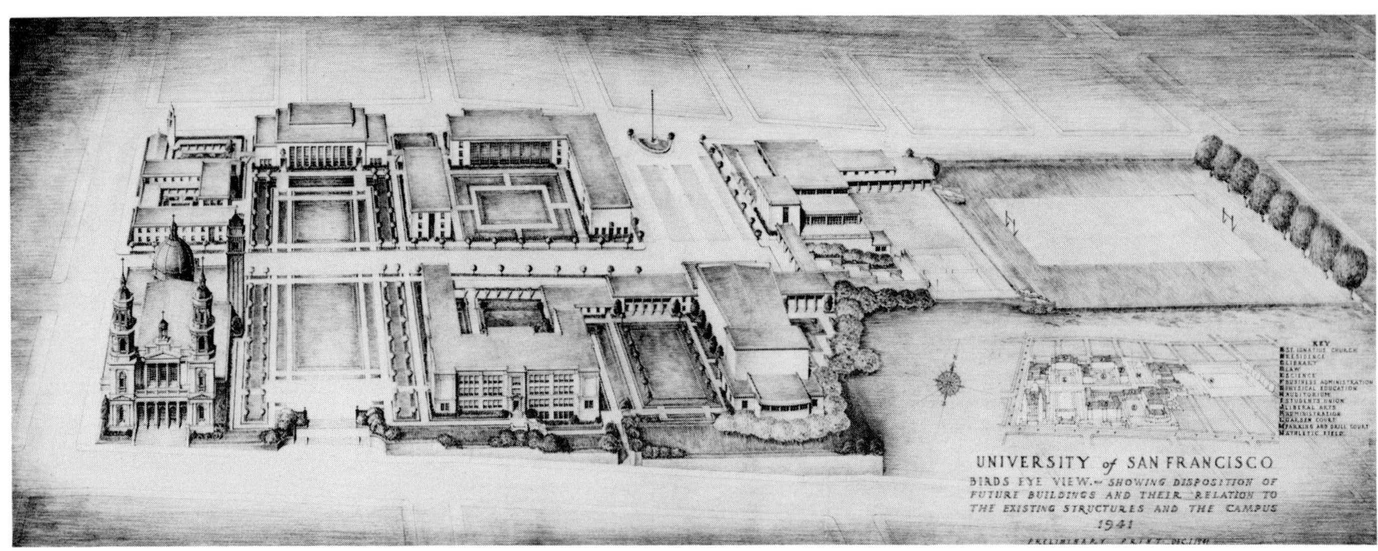

60. UNIVERSITY OF SAN FRANCISCO, San Francisco, 1941 (Architect's Rendering). The first drawing, an aerial view of Campus Development, made in 1941. Facility needs envisioned at the time changed dramatically in the years to come.

61. UNIVERSITY OF SAN FRANCISCO, San Francisco, (Courtesy of Pacific Telephone & Telegraph Company). Aerial view, Main Campus and Lone Mountain Campus. The buildings, of contemporary design, bow in reverence to St. Ignatius Church, the campus cornerstone, whose twin spires, dome and campanile in the Spanish Renaissance style dominate the hilltop campus.

62. UNIVERSITY OF SAN FRANCISCO, 1967 (Joshua Freiwald). Gillson and Hayes-Healy Residence Halls named to honor benefactors.

63. UNIVERSITY OF SAN FRANCISCO (Joshua Freiwald). Hayes-Healy Hall. Student Court at Main Entrance.

64. UNIVERSITY OF SAN FRANCISCO, 1959 (Joshua Freiwald). Xavier Hall—the Faculty Residence, Gleeson Library—in honor of former President Father Richard Gleeson S.J., Harney Science Center—named to honor Charles E. Harney, University Trustee and Benefactor.

65. UNIVERSITY OF SAN FRANCISCO, 1966, (Joshua Freiwald). Student Center—Robert Howard's "Phoenix", symbolic of the University and the City.

66. *UNIVERSITY OF SAN FRANCISCO, 1968 (Joshua Freiwald). Cowell Hall—the School of Nursing, named for the Benefactor, the Cowell Foundation.*

67. *UNIVERSITY OF SAN FRANCISCO, 1961 (Joshua Freiwald). Rotunda of Library, Kendrick Hall—the School of Law—named to honor Charles Kendrick, University Trustee and Benefactor.*

68. UNIVERSITY OF CALIFORNIA MEDICAL CENTER, San Francisco, 1956 (Moulin Studios). Aerial View.

69. UNIVERSITY OF CALIFORNIA MEDICAL CENTER, 1956 (Joshua Freiwald). From Golden Gate Park—the taller building, far left, is the Herbert C. Moffit Teaching Hospital, with Medical Sciences adjoining. In the foreground, (across Parnassus Avenue) is Millberry Union.

UNIVERSITY OF CALIFORNIA MEDICAL CENTER

Work for the UNIVERSITY OF CALIFORNIA MEDICAL CENTER in San Francisco began in our office in the early 1930s. The 500 bed Herbert C. Moffitt Teaching Hospital was in the programming, planning and building stages for nearly a quarter of a century, construction alone requiring five years (1950-1955), due to shortage and control of materials during the Korean War. The ultimate Center, when completed (perhaps not until the late years of this century) was inconceivable in the 1930s and 1940s, such being the unbelievable medical advancements of our times. However, our Teaching Hospital and the adjoining Medical Sciences, (Blanchard and Maher, Architects), were the first "new" units of the now world renowned Center.

The weekly meetings with the Heads of the Medical Departments started early in the 1930s and continued into the 1940s. I attended these meetings with Tim and this was my earliest experience in witnessing the building needs of a major hospital being developed "by Committee."

Of course I was in awe, Tim to a lesser degree, of the company with whom we sat at the conference table. They were the most eminent doctors in their specialties, impressive in manner and appearance, thoroughly convinced as to the needs of their respective departments, and each resistive (rightfully) to pre-emption by others. Never to be forgotten are Doctors Naffziger, Kerr, Abbott, Hinman, Smythe, Fleming, Deamer, and Tracy, Head of Nursing. There was great sympathy for the Committee Chairman (several over the years) whose unenviable task it was to bring agreement among such strong personalities.

Equally important was the battle in the State Legislature for greater recognition and appropriation, and this was mainly the success of Jim Corey, Vice-President of Finance for the University, under the direction of President Robert Sproul whose voice still rings as I remember the Dedication in 1955.

The art of programming has become more sophisticated since those early years and we now have many more tools in this demanding task.

Roscoe Weaver, Robert Evans and Jack Wagstaff were planners and architects of the University who worked with us, and it was interesting to me that long before Jack became involved his father had been in our office working on the very earliest schematics of the Hospital. A decade or more before that, he had directed the production of the drawings for the War Memorial Opera House, this at the time I was starting in the office of Bakewell & Brown.

Time and generations were bridged during this Hospital project, not surprising when one considers that nearly 25 years elapsed from the start of our work until completion of the building, an era in which both World War II and the Korean War had their tragic place.

The Millberry Union at the Medical Center was completed in 1958. This we called "The Combined Structure" during planning and construction because of the varied facilities therein—lounges, dining, recreation, swimming, gymnasium, housing for interns and student nurses, and a 575 car public garage. To our dismay a planned outdoor recreation terrace over the parking roof of the lower garage has not been constructed to this time. Overlooking Golden Gate Park with the towers of the Golden Gate Bridge looming in the distance, the terrace would afford a very welcome respite on campus.

70. UNIVERSITY OF CALIFORNIA MEDICAL CENTER, 1958 (Joshua Freiwald). Robert Howard's "Tree of Knowledge" adorns the fireplace in the Lounge of Millberry Union.

THE COMMUNITY COLLEGE OF SAN FRANCISCO

The SAN FRANCISCO COMMUNITY COLLEGE DISTRICT was formed in 1970, thus joining the City College of San Francisco and the Adult/Occupational Division of the Unified School District. The Community College District has its own elected Board of Governors and is an entity separate from the Unified School District.

The progress and services of this institution have been remarkable by every indicator, but my thought is to note our involvement in its development, and this concerns City College in Balboa Park.

The San Francisco Junior College was started in 1935 with Dr. Archie Cloud, its initiator, as President. The City College site in Balboa Park was first occupied in 1940 with Tim as the College Architect. The three permanent buildings completed in 1940 and 1941 were the all-purpose Academic Building, now converted to Sciences, the Men's and Women's Gymnasia and the Athletic Field.

Cloud Hall-East, constructed in 1979, is the eleventh permanent structure for which we served as Architects.

It is noteworthy to consider City College and the University of San Francisco. For approximately the same number of years, we have served these institutions and are continuing to do so.

There is no greater challenge than to plan for growing institutions. Initially, a Master Plan must be conceived, based upon so many unknowns.

As time goes on, needs change; population, enrollments, people, purposes, and all factors dealing with education are constantly changing. Flexibility, an over-used word, is nevertheless a must; options and alternatives must be possible. Yet through the years and with all the growing, there should always be a sense of completeness as it applies to the particular time. Every student, whatever his particular time may be, should not be told or have the feeling that his time is too soon; if only a few years hence, then so much more would be available.

How easy it is to say these things, but how difficult to accomplish. Seldom is the opportunity presented to design and complete in one fell swoop a complex of buildings or a complete facility, based upon established needs. And then there is the matter of design, or more precisely, how to come to terms with external architecture, when it encompasses 3, 4 and 5 decades. Here in our firm we believe this to be true: design in the contemporary using the best technology, change materials and methods of construction as best fit, but when so doing, let there be not a clash but a compatibility between new and old. There is of course the direct opposite view: Each to its own, delicate or brutal. Enough, for this question will never be agreed upon in any event.

How can we think of City College without speaking of personalities? Archie Cloud, its founder and first President, was one of the University of California students who stole the Axe from Stanford, a story that will be retold for all time. He was a great man, a great educator, kindly, full of fun and one loved by all.

When I graduated from Mission High School in 1924, for some reason I was chosen to make one of the student speeches. I asked Bob Chase, my "home room" teacher (with whom I played tennis almost daily, and who later became Principal at Balboa High), what possibly could I talk about. He said, "I can't tell you, but you go see Dr. Cloud, the Assistant Superintendent of Schools. He'll give you some very good advice." I did, meeting Dr. Cloud for the first time, and was most kindly advised.

I cannot recollect meeting Dr. Cloud again until we started work on City College in the '30s. He, of course, was a good friend of Tim. When Cloud Hall was to be dedicated in 1954, Dr. Louis G. Conlan, then President, succeeding Dr. Cloud in 1949, asked me if I would say something at the Dedication Program. Whom did I turn to? Dr. Cloud, of course. Even more so than 30 years previously, he helped with all his time and patience.

At the time we were working more directly with Dr. Louis "Dutch" Conlan, who was President for 21 years until his retirement in 1970 and in whose regime City College became one of the great Junior Colleges of our State, free of strife in the turbulent '60s and justly so because of his firmness coupled with kindness and understanding. With the growth of the College it was he, with Drs. Harry Buttimer and Louis Batmale and, of course, the Board, and indeed the City, who made the far reaching decisions for the future Community College and the College District.

A great quarterback at St. Mary's at its football zenith, "Dutch" Conlan now is still the master golfer. John and I know him as an intimate friend, and we cherish this very highly. The Educational Services Building, completed in 1968, is named in his honor.

Upon Dr. Conlan's retirement, Dr. Louis F. Batmale became Chancellor and Dr. Harry Buttimer the President of City College. This was shortly after the formation of the San Francisco Community College District, an entity separate from the Unified School District. Dr. Buttimer, after serving several years left to become President of Chabot Junior College.

Drs. Kenneth S. Washington and Calvin Dellefield were appointed by the Governing Board as President of the City College and the Community College Centers.

Hopefully, Dr. Batmale, recently retired Chancellor, will write a comprehensive history of this remarkable College District, with a total enrollment of approximately 100,000, of which 16,000 are day-time and 10,000 night-time students at the City College in Balboa Park; the others in the Community College Centers throughout the City.

71. THE COMMUNITY COLLEGE OF SAN FRANCISCO, 1942 San Francisco, (Gabriel Moulin). The first permanent all-purpose Academic Building, later converted to Sciences.

72. THE COMMUNITY COLLEGE OF SAN FRANCISCO, 1954 (Joshua Freiwald). Cloud Hall, from the practice field, with the Academic Building behind.

73. THE COMMUNITY COLLEGE OF SAN FRANCISCO, 1971 (Joshua Freiwald). Creative Arts Building.

74. LELAND STANFORD JUNIOR UNIVERSITY, (Courtesy of Stanford University). The Inner Quad in 1891. The 12 original buildings enclose a huge courtyard (250 by 600 feet). Today towering trees rise from the eight planting islands.

LELAND STANFORD JUNIOR UNIVERSITY

LELAND STANFORD JUNIOR UNIVERSITY is very special in our hearts for many reasons. So much history, so many stories of this great institution have been written. From our own so definitely imprinted experiences, I may dare to add a bit while reflecting on our work.

Looking at a colored aerial photo of the Campus hanging in our conference room is always thrilling. Harry L. Sanders, recently retired Director of Planning, once told me that when J. E. Wallace Sterling, former President and now Chancellor of the University, first approached the Campus via Palm Drive, he looked over the Oval to the Quad and the golden hills beyond; he stood in awe and said, this is for me. I cannot quote the words; Wally would have said it so beautifully, and I understand such a thought coming from a giant among men. Is it strange that I say "Wally"? I do not find it so. A truly great man, the most sensitive, kind and friendly giant of all.

If people seem to be as vivid in my thoughts as grounds and buildings, so be it. It is people, Trustees, Administrators, Faculty, Students, Alumni, Friends and all others, on and off Campus, who make all this possible. Alf Brandin, former Vice-President for Business, was a leader in the concepts of preservation and development, all the while adhering to the strict requirements set down by Leland Stanford when he deeded the vast acreage and built the first building; and when one received approbation from Alf, a very great satisfaction was felt.

Architecturally, above all preserve the Quad; make its stone walls earthquake-proof; gut the insides to suit present needs. Respect the past. Create courts and vistas of intimacy and grandeur. Landscape abundantly and save the grand trees that could never be replaced. Don't misunderstand: Money is not wasted or spread indiscriminately, but neither is it the sole criterion. Finding the proper balance is not easy, but those who serve Stanford come to this balance more often than not.

In the early 1950s, we received the commission to do Florence Moore Hall, a women students' residence. This was due in great part to Ted Spencer, a friend knowledgeable of our office for many years. His recommendations I know had much to do with my appointment. He was the head of the Planning Department, close to both the Trustees and former President

75. LELAND STANFORD JUNIOR UNIVERSITY, Palo Alto, California, 1956 (Joshua Freiwald). Florence Moore Hall. One of the informal courts; each of the seven 50-student units has a court to call its own.

Donald Tresidder. He did much distinguished work at Yosemite Park as well as at Stanford.

Florence Moore Hall was particularly interesting since it had been decided that in lieu of many students in one building, it would be preferable to limit the number in one building to fifty women. Seven units, each with its own lounges and dining rooms, were to be grouped around a central service. Each unit was to be otherwise completely independent with its own amenities and outdoor spaces.

Control to all units was centralized and protection for the students was such that no living quarters were to be at ground level; so the buildings were in great part open at grade with covered walks through and connecting all units. To indicate changing concepts in University living, just some years ago we added living quarters in the covered ground areas and the Hall is now coeducational! It was a good concept in the beginning and is no less successful or pleasing now.

While the original Florence Moore Hall was in the design stages, John was soon to enter a University to start a career in Architecture. While at Lincoln High School, he was on the all—city basketball team and consequently had some options as to University choice, among them Stanford. On one of our strolls on Campus, I asked Ted Spencer for a candid opinion and his reply was to the effect that while some other universities might have greater recognition as to Architectural Schools, this was more than compensated for by the nature of Stanford as a whole, and this we found to be true. John received his BA at Stanford in 1960 and then entered our office.

While watching John at Stanford, at work and at play, I very often thought of what I had missed and was glad that he had a fine education and a great time as well. There was no big decision to be made when he expressed his desire to come into the office. I was very happy and everyone in the office, knowing him well, was the same. This has never changed, and I consider myself most fortunate that I am now his partner. The Stanford connection continues and the pleasure and pride in this fact cannot be overstated.

Almost concurrently with Florence Moore Hall, we associated with Spencer and Ambrose on the Dinkelspiel Memorial Auditorium which seats 730 and was then quite unique with a rounded forestage projecting well into the audience; with only 15 rows of seating, there is intimacy between audience and stage. We again had the fortune of working with and for Lloyd Dinkelspiel, a Trustee President who some years later was followed by one of his law Partners, Richard Guggenhime, in the same position.

The thread weaves on. Sidney Ehrman,

76. LELAND STANFORD JUNIOR UNIVERSITY, 1957 (Joshua Freiwald). Dinkelspiel Memorial Auditorium. The Entrance Facade. A design of less formality, appropriate to the al fresco plaza and the Tresidder Union which is opposite the Auditorium.

77. LELAND STANFORD JUNIOR UNIVERSITY, (Joshua Freiwald). Dinkelspiel Memorial Auditorium. Intimacy, with only 15 rows of seating and a stage and adjustable orchestra pit protruding into the seating area.

Florence McAuliffe, Lloyd Dinkelspiel, all now gone but Dick Guggenhime who is leading on in the law firm of Heller, Ehrman, White and McAuliffe; his partner, Robert C. Harris, son of the late Larry Harris. (I well remember that on the death of my brother Tim, it was Larry Harris who called shortly thereafter with regard to a job and thus became my first "new" client.)

We remodeled the interiors of several Quad wings as well as others outside the Quad, including the Law Annex Wing, the Food Research Institute at Encina Hall and Student Services in the old Union.

Going back prior to these: In 1960 the Ford Foundation gave $25 million to Stanford, providing Stanford brought the total to $100 million. This set the three year PACE program, the Plan of Action for a Challenging Era. Other annual giving programs continued during the PACE campaign. In this year, Wally Sterling asked Gardner Dailey, John Warnecke and me to lunch. His question was: Would we be willing to serve as an Architectural Advisory Committee, meeting with the Planning Department and/or Administration when called, who in turn of course reported to the Trustees and Trustees Building Committee.

Our task was to be purely advisory; comment upon Architectural-Planning ideas and presentation; in general, lend a hand to a very able Planning Department who might, by our contributions, feel a greater security in their evaluations and recommendations. We, of course, were honored and unhesitatingly accepted. Only one suggestion was made—to include Tommy Church, the great Landscape Architect. Wally agreed immediately; and of the four, Jack Warnecke and I still serve, Ernie Kump replacing Gardner on his death, and Tommy recently retiring for health reasons. Upon Harry Sanders' recent retirement, the Committee has been augmented with several other members.

In our design of the Graduate School of Business which flanks the Quad to the southeast, it was the aim to complement the primary facade of the Quad, to respect and contribute to the environment, and yet reflect an independence of its own nature and time without pretense or affectation. The building has many major components reflecting the unique programs developed by Ernest C. Arbuckle who, after serving ten years as Dean of the School, resigned to become the Chairman of the Board of Wells Fargo and Company; he was the driving

78. LELAND STANFORD JUNIOR UNIVERSITY, 1966 (Phil Fein). The Graduate School of Business. Looking down from the Hoover Library.

79. LELAND STANFORD JUNIOR UNIVERSITY, 1966 (Joshua Freiwald). The Graduate School of Business. The main facade, facing the Oval.

80. LELAND STANFORD JUNIOR UNIVERSITY, (Joshua Freiwald). Graduate School of Business. The rear facade, less formal. The interplay of tile roofs, the deep shadows, the color of warm sandstone—this is the vocabulary, taken from the character of the Quadrangle.

force in bringing the School to the top in our country, standing alongside the Harvard Graduate School of Business. I must also remember that in the main court of the school stands "Flamebirds," the work of renowned sculptor Francis Stahly, a gift of my very dear friend William Lowe.

The Center for Biological Sciences flanks the Quad to the northeast and was completed in 1967, one year after the Graduate School of Business. As with the Graduate School of Business, the particular Quad environment of arcades, courts, warm color and tile roofs is reflected. Not in the Romanesque style of the Quad, the new flanking buildings are nevertheless, by reason of utmost concern to scale and proportion, in harmony.

81. LELAND STANFORD JUNIOR UNIVERSITY, 1967 (Joshua Freiwald). Center for Biological Sciences. The facade facing the Oval with the Quad on the left, through the palm trees.

82. LELAND STANFORD JUNIOR UNIVERSITY, (Joshua Freiwald). Center for Biological Sciences. The teaching wing from the court. The bridges connect to the research wing. Directly across the Oval from the School of Business, the Center has a similar vocabulary, a character respectful of the Quad.

The Stanford Medical School and Hospital, dedicated in 1959, was designed by Edward Durrell Stone. Lack of funds did not permit completion of the first step of this Center. Clinical Sciences Research Wing, between the Hospital Pavilion and the Medical School, was added in 1966 in the original Ed Stone character and here we associated with him. He had been a close friend of Tim, and therefore known by me for many years; having lost to Ed in the original med school-hospital architect selection process, I valued this association highly.

To play a role at Stanford is indeed a privilege. Meeting and knowing those who have guided and are guiding its destiny is a very rewarding experience. Dr. Richard Lyman, President, and all of the Stanford family have a sense of purpose which is to bring forth the best, to foresee the future and to lead, not follow.

We received a copy of Dr. Richard W. Lyman's "REFLECTIONS ON THE SUCCESS OF THE CAMPAIGN FOR STANFORD," dated May 10, 1977, which followed by just a few days the press news that Stanford's five year campaign to raise $300 million had in fact surpassed its goal.

Dr. Lyman, in pondering the success of the Campaign, attributes it beyond all else to the respect for Stanford's commitments to EXCELLENCE and to INDEPENDENCE. His "REFLECTIONS" will take a significant place in our library and could well be read by all who are concerned with our future.

Subsequent to this writing Dr. Lyman tendered his resignation and became President of the Rockefeller Foundation. Dr. Donald Kennedy, who had left his position as Director of Biological Sciences at Stanford to serve in Washington as Director of the Food & Drug Administration was selected as the new President of the University.

COLLEGE OF THE HOLY NAMES

The COLLEGE OF THE HOLY NAMES, a women's college organized and administered by the Sisters of the Holy Names, is located on the western slope of the Oakland Hills on a 40-acre site. Founded in 1868, for 89 years until its new campus was dedicated in 1957, it had been on the shores of Lake Merritt, on the site of what is now Kaiser Center.

The steepness of the slope motivated a linear plan with a peripheral entrance-service road. The composition affords sweeping panoramic views of the Bay, and the San Francisco-Marin peninsulas from San Jose to Mount Tamalpais. Of restrained contemporary architecture, the Chapel and Campanile high on the site dominate against a background of eucalyptus trees which serve as a buffer from the residential area beyond.

Academic Facilities, Library, Administration, Student Center, Student and Sister Housing, Gymnasium and Pool and the Chapel constituted the first buildings. Only the Auditorium was lacking to make it a complete facility; the Gymnasium has served for this purpose. We added two student residences, another Classroom-Sciences building and an Art Center in later years.

To a very large degree, here at Holy Names we were able to do at once a complete campus, as opposed to a lengthy building-by-building progression. This opportunity does not often present itself. The search for unity and character representing the spirit of the Sisters was challenging and rewarding.

Again we speak of people, in this case the Sisters with whom we worked. Leff Miller and I went to the Sisters' Home in Los Gatos for the selection interview. As we left, each had the

83. COLLEGE OF THE HOLY NAMES, Oakland, 1958 (Joshua Freiwald) Panoramic Campus view. Basically a two level composition: the upper level with Faculty and Student Residence Facilities, the lower with Academic Facilities. By reason of elevation above a freeway and the City, and the buffer eucalyptus groves, the Campus, with courts and abundant landscaping is quiet and secluded. The horizontals of roof fascias converge to the Chapel and Tower which feature the composition, and symbolize the Spirit.

84. COLLEGE OF THE HOLY NAMES, 1958 (Joshua Freiwald). Chapel, with Cross atop the Bell Tower.

same thought: We must have this job, just to work in the glow of such goodness! So it came to be, and I can think of no job experience wherein we looked forward to our meetings with greater anticipation. From Mother Superior and all, we received only kindness and consideration.

It became the task of Sister Emily Marie to work with us throughout the entire project, from programming through construction. While many others were closely involved, our constant coordinator was Sister Emily. Her keen mind and patience were an inspiration.

Words are inadequate, but each telephone call or request from the College of the Holy Names brings forth again the pleasure and satisfaction of a most rewarding experience.

85. COLLEGE OF THE HOLY NAMES, 1960 (Joshua Freiwald). Unit of Student Residence Complex.

86. COLLEGE OF THE HOLY NAMES, 1958 (Joshua Freiwald). James D. Kennedy Memorial Arts Center.

87. THE CALIFORNIA ACADEMY OF SCIENCES, San Francisco, 1975 (Lloyd Ullberg; Courtesy of the California Academy of Sciences). Wattis Hall of Man.

88. THE CALIFORNIA ACADEMY OF SCIENCES, (Rob Super). The McBean-Peterson Galleries.

CALIFORNIA ACADEMY OF SCIENCES

To say our work at the CALIFORNIA ACADEMY OF SCIENCES in Golden Gate Park has been interesting is an understatement. It started quite sedately and without great complication with a Library addition to the east of the Planetarium. This was in 1959.

In the 1960s, a Cowell Foundation grant made possible a long awaited connecting Hall between the two flanking Halls, thus creating a unity of composition and a strong visual identity for the Academy on the Concourse Facade. An Academy Court would be created in place of the open court with its individual entrances to North American and African Halls, to Steinhart Aquarium and to the Morrison Planetarium. In addition to providing a large Hall as the connection, it then created a single, controllable public entrance and information center to the entire Academy.

Lewis Hobart had been the Architect of the flanking American and African Halls of the Academy and also had made studies of a complete facade showing a central classic colonnade fronting a solid mass.

It was our thought that it should be a "see-through" Hall so that from the Concourse exterior one would see the Court beyond. Our first studies carried this concept through a structural steel frame, with full glass and thin bronze columns, a large concourse Academy Plaza, the feature of which was to be Robert Howard's beautiful large granite "Whales" with its water sprays and pool.

This was a bold concept, perhaps too bold. As all San Franciscans know, Golden Gate Park, as it should be, is sacred, and anything done therein undergoes the closest scrutiny. Naturally the Music Concourse, with the Band Stand, and the flanking Academy and the DeYoung Museum is of primary concern in the world renowned Park. Our first concept was therefore rightfully considered in depth by the Academy, the Park and Recreation Commission and the Art Commission. The consensus was adverse to our concept and, although disappointed, we did understand the concern and were by no means obdurate nor insensible to the feelings expressed.

89. THE CALIFORNIA ACADEMY OF SCIENCES, 1975 (Lloyd Ullberg; Courtesy of the California Academy of Sciences). Steinhart Aquarium. The GHC Meyer Fish Roundabout.

Much study was given, resulting in a finely textured pre-cast concrete system clearly relating to the classic proportions of the existing wings. A large Portico is featured and its walls are actually non-walls of glass with the Court facade all glass, thus providing the vistas of the Academy and the Court, interior and exterior, old and new. Robert Howard's "Whales" and pool are in the Academy Court and a sunken court leads to a lower Dining Area.

On the basis of appropriateness as a contemporary addition, thoroughly consistent and har-

90. THE CALIFORNIA ACADEMY OF SCIENCES, 1967 (Joshua Freiwald). Cowell Hall, across Music Concourse. As built.

91. THE CALIFORNIA ACADEMY OF SCIENCES Architect's model of early concept of Cowell Hall.

monious with earlier classic design, Cowell Hall won a National Award.

Does this prove that our original concept could not have evolved as successfully? Not necessarily, but it does indicate that a very strong personal statement is not the only answer; and when adding to, or designing near the old and revered, give careful consideration to a harmonious blending.

In the 1970s, the Academy presented another challenge. The rear of the complex toward Middle Drive of the Park had long been unsightly with an aura of backside or the rear of a complex. Service to the Academy, poor parking, undistinguished facades and general unsightliness prevailed.

Again, under the Director of the Academy Dr. George E. Lindsay and the Board of Trustees perhaps the most ambitious project in its 123-year history took place. This was particularly so because of the multiple facets included in the program. These mainly included the Wattis Hall of Man and Wattis Gallery, the Departments of Entomology and Botany, the Athol McBean and Patricia Price Galleries, and the G.H.C. Meyer Foundation Fish Roundabout. With these, underground service as well as a staff garage were provided, and very importantly, a secondary public entrance to the Academy was provided from Middle Drive, relieving congestion on the Concourse.

As with Cowell Hall, all study came under the most careful scrutiny by the civic authorities.

The solution evolved with three new structures: The Entrance Gallery (McBean and Price Galleries), the Wattis Hall of Man (with Botany and Entomology on upper floors) and the Meyer Foundation Fish Roundabout. The original rear facade of the Academy is completely screened by the new elements, each being technically challenging and the combining even more so.

The Roundabout, for example, is an extraordinary mid-ocean experience. From the Aquarium main level where you are introduced graphically and pictorially to the open sea, you ascend a graceful spiral ramp to the inside of a unique 100,000 gallon ring-tank, surrounded by schooling pelagic fishes, an experience likened to a deep sea dive.

This project is not another Cowell Hall, which highlights the Concourse facade. Here the natural park environment has been preserved and enhanced. The Art Commission, in its approval, described the project as "architecture and landscape . . . married into a composition of striking interest and beauty."

These additions add luster and new facilities to one of the most renowned natural science museums of the world.

92. THE CALIFORNIA ACADEMY OF SCIENCES, 1967 (Joshua Freiwald). Court Facade of Cowell Hall with Robert Howard's "Whales".

93. *WALTER REED GENERAL HOSPITAL, Washington D.C., 1977 (Peter Xiques). Main Facade. The Plaza with cherry tree-lined walks is the roof of the 1,000 car subsurface parking structure. One of the earliest design decisions was the elimination of multi-story above-grade parking structures as proposed in site studies by former planners. The low-rise hospital is dictated by the height restriction in our Capital City, a restriction which makes the Capital one of the beautiful cities of the world.*

JOINT VENTURES

It was noted earlier that we were engaged in programming and concepts for Mt. Zion Hospital in San Francisco at the time of Tim's death. Shortly thereafter, David Zellerbach, Chairman of the Hospital Board, asked me to consider associating with a firm in New York and mentioned the name. Knowing our work load, he made the suggestion in the most kindly manner. I understood the situation and replied that I knew the firm by reputation (no need to mention the name), but nothing about its principals or present status. Would not a more suitable and mutually advantageous association result with a firm I did know, i.e., Skidmore, Owings & Merrill of New York and Chicago. (I was thinking of an afternoon not too long before when "Skid" had been in our office and he, Tim and I had dinner and an evening at the Stage Door Canteen.)

With Zellerbach's consent, I flew to New York for a meeting with Skid and Nat Owings in their office. We had a good meeting and in a week or so, Nat came out to San Francisco to meet Zellerbach. We three had a drink at the Stock Exchange Lunch Club and all was settled in short order. SOM opened an office across from us on Market Street—they had told me in New York they had been considering this. We did the work in that office and Nat, John Rodgers and John Lord King of SOM became my good friends.

Charles Blyth, Chairman of the Board at Mills Hospital, asked if we would make the same arrangement with respect to our work there, and this was done.

It could be said then, that I opened the door quite nicely for SOM. I could dwell on the ifs and buts forever, all to no purpose.

In 1957, our office was commissioned by the Corps of Engineers to do Schematic and Preliminary Plans for a 1000-1500 bed hospital and support facilities at Fort Ord, California.

Concurrently, Stone, Marraccini and Patterson of San Francisco was commissioned to do an "Advance Planning Report" for a 1000-1500 bed hospital at the Oakland Naval Base, California.

Neither of these projects went beyond the Preliminary plans stage, the Department of Defense going into a review stage of military hospitals, generally. The projects, however, had a vital influence on our future activity.

In 1962, the Department of Defense had resolved its thinking and determined upon a new 650 bed hospital at the Oakland Naval Base, and a 550 bed hospital for Letterman General in the Presidio of San Francisco. The Department further resolved that the two facilities' (although designed to independent requirements of the Navy and the Army, respectively) contractural control and management would be in the hands of the Twelfth Naval District, San Bruno, California; further, one Architect-Engineer entity should be selected for both projects.

Since Doug Stone and I had enjoyed mutual respect for many years, it seemed good sense that we should form a Joint Venture in the application for selection as Architect-Engineer. If we did not do this, one or the other was definitely out, and conceivably both. Considering the two projects we felt so close to, that thought was unbearable. We formed our Joint Venture and we were selected.

We again expanded our quarters at 580 Market Street and there joined our staffs for the accomplishment of the work.

Each of the projects presented its challenges and the solutions are unique in response to the requirements. Hospital planning is not one of the easier facets of the profession. Medical advances in our time have been tremendous, of which we are all aware. This alone is not what is challenging. There are many factors, and as in all of architecture, the human element is of utmost concern.

But these memoirs will not attempt to define that which makes a hospital good or not so good. Rather, I would recall circumstances at Letterman—all of us were so vitally concerned with its environmental impact: close to the Bay, near the revered Palace of Fine Arts; obstruction of vistas from the neighborhood hills; indeed, obstruction of hillsides from the Bay; saving of trees, mass, color. All the tools were required to arrive at a solution which satisfactorily answered these concerns, and yet did not impair a sound, functional, well-planned medical facility. Both hospitals were successfully completed and dedicated in 1969.

During their construction, actually in mid-1967, our same Joint Venture was commissioned to do the 440-bed Silas B. Hayes Hospital at Ft. Ord, Monterey, California; this hospital was dedicated in December, 1971, a very accelerated time frame set by the Government, and met.

But there is yet to tell the climax of the work of this same Joint Venture, and that is the Walter Reed General Hospital in Washington, D.C.

The Walter Reed Medical Center is the Army fountainhead in the Department of Defense health care system. The major hospital facilities on the Center were not only housed in "Building No. 1," a five-story, 700′ long Georgian Colonial brick building, but in many other separated structures, some arcade connected, others not. Many concepts by various architects over a period of many years were planned for its replacement, none coming to fruition.

In 1969 the Department of Defense, with the approval of the Congress, delegated the Corps of

94. LETTERMAN GENERAL HOSPITAL, PRESIDIO, San Francisco, 1967 (Joshua Freiwald). Patient Solarium, toward Bay and Golden Gate.

95. LETTERMAN GENERAL HOSPITAL, (Joshua Freiwald). Main Entrance Facade.

96. OAKLAND NAVAL HOSPITAL, Oakland, 1967 (Joshua Freiwald).

97. SILAS B. HAYES HOSPITAL, FT. ORD, Monterey, 1968 (Joshua Freiwald).

Engineers through the Baltimore, Maryland District to reactivate the building of a new Walter Reed General Hospital and to therefore select an Architect-Engineer. Of the hundreds of applicants over the whole country we were selected. This we considered a singular honor, for this commission was the largest and most prestigious project for either partner and the Joint Venture.

To say that the design of this 1300-bed hospital, dedicated to patient care, teaching and research, with well over a million square feet (not including an under-plaza parking garage for more than 1000 cars), involved greater intensive study than any previous project is a very fair statement. Surely each partner of the Joint Venture had individually designed large hospital projects, but none encompassed the factors prevalent here. The history is worthy of a book and I will not attempt a condensed version, but only some reflections.

Perhaps, in retrospect, the factors I think of are in truth similar to those one encounters on many projects. Here, however, even though of the same nature, their impact was magnified to the greatest extent. You do not conceive, plan and make determinations for such a facility in the Capitol City of our land, on the Medical Center of the United States Army, without soon realizing that all eyes are upon you; only the most intensive analysis and research will find acceptance and approval.

Think of the client. It is the President (there is a Presidential Suite), the Congress, the Department of Defense, the Office of the Surgeon General, the Corps of Engineers with the North Atlantic Division and the Baltimore District, and the U.S. Army from the highest ranking officers to the privates, and their dependents. Then consider the Capitol Planning Commission and the Fine Arts Commission who must review and approve. The height limit of buildings in the Capitol and, of course, every environmental factor is considered to the ultimate degree.

Certainly, one would be inhuman to embark upon such a mission without trepidation and grave concern. Fortunately, all involved are human beings with a common cause, and patience and perseverance accomplish wonders.

Never have we been involved in a project of such complexity. We came to understand why

98. WALTER REED GENERAL HOSPITAL, Washington D.C., 1977 (Peter Xiques). Patient Court. In-patient beds are on the upper three floors, fifth, sixth and seventh. This is one of four large courts, all at the fifth floor level.

99. WALTER REED GENERAL HOSPITAL, (Peter Xiques). Main patient lobby.

the building of the new hospital had been under consideration for so many years and why concept after concept had been proposed and rejected. Well over ten million dollars was expended on what was termed "Interim Facilities." This described the temporary relocation of the myriad facilities which were housed in the many buildings on the new hospital site, all of which were to be demolished. Without graphics, words alone cannot describe this complicated planning. There was no other solution if the hospital was to remain operational, and this was mandatory. I truly cannot remember the number of "bid packages" that we prepared for interim facilities, all before demolition and site clearing for the new hospital.

Nor will I attempt a description of the design of the hospital in these recollections. When we made presentations, many hours—full days—and drawings without number were required. All who had a part in this great experience will long remember, for it was a once in a lifetime opportunity.

The project, I feel confident, will take its place as the foremost medical facility of its kind.

Sadly, Doug Stone and Syl Marraccini have been gone for some years. Norman Patterson, President of the Stone, Marraccini, Patterson Corporation, has been my co-principal on the work of this Joint Venture. Our work together has produced great mutual respect, admiration and friendship. This extends through the personnel of both firms, and this is noteworthy for, believe me, Joint Ventures are not so always.

In the early part of 1957, Architects-Engineers were selected for a new Naval Air Station at Lemoore, California.

Urbahn, Brayton and Burrows of New York City, now Max O. Urbahn and Associates, and our firm formed a Joint Venture and were selected to do the "Administration Area" of the Station. The project involved the site planning of the 200-acre "Administration Area" and included the design of all buildings thereon, including Administration, Enlisted Men's Barracks and Mess, Bachelor Officer Quarters and Mess, Club Facilities, Welfare and Recreation Centers, Hospital and the many related ancillary facilities; total of the separately packaged construction contracts involved $26,000,000 and it was completed in 1961.

Expansion of our quarters at 580 Market Street permitted the joining of personnel from our two architectural firms and all work was accomplished here.

This Joint Venture (which actually preceded our Joint Venture with Stone, Marraccini and Patterson) was most successful. One does not lightly form a Joint Venture. The principals and primary personnel must not only know and respect the capabilities of each other, but must be sure of compatibility. We were not new to each other and were clearly aware that all conditions were most favorable. Indeed, Richard Brayton spent many months in San Francisco, as did Philip Moyer, then their Administrative Director, now Executive Vice President of Max Urbahn and Associates.

The personnel of our two firms meshed ideally and enduring friendships prevail to this day.

Isadore Thompson, Structural Engineer of San Francisco who has worked with our office for 25 or more years, was the Structural Engineer for all our Joint Venture work. This is an opportune time in these reflections to pay tribute to Tommy, whose experience, versatility and innovative thinking has meant so much to our work.

100. U.S. NAVAL AIR STATION, Lemoore, 1961. Aerial view—Administrative and Personnel Support Complex. The Complex includes all station facilities with the exception of hangars and attendant operational facilities.

FRIENDS TO REMEMBER

To here, one could believe that our military work was primarily Joint Venture work. Before those events occurred, we were involved in much work for the military and continue to be. Projects need not be named; enough to say the work is always interesting and very diversified.

Governmental, and military work particularly, requires patience and perseverance. The agencies are numerous on any project and it is the nature of the military branches that personnel change frequently. Communication may seem, and is at times, circuitous and time consuming. Manuals, technical bulletins and directives are constantly amended and updated; to some architect-engineer firms, the "red tape" must seem very burdensome. To perform well, this must be accepted and dealt with as expeditiously as possible.

Those who do perform well are those who not only understand the "system," but those who realize the value of human relationships. Computers are among the many tools, but the human being is the directing element, and we are working for and with people. It is this that dominates my thoughts, and although some contacts are transitory, there are so many that are not. There are those I shall hopefully never forget; but to be certain, in the years to come I will merely have to refer to these pages and my memory will be refreshed. To do this authentically and to avoid omissions and forgetfulness, records and files should be searched. I have not the patience for this and since this is not a documentation, my recollections must suffice.

To the uninitiated, the signatory parties to a Military AE Contract are the Chief Officer of the Project District and the Architect. However, the program of needs, the budget, etc., are established in Washington and we therefore are involved with many "Washington people" as well as the particular District. These people may be military or civilian.

Our early work reminds me forcibly of the late Surgeon General of the Army, Leonard Heaton. Mutual friendships paved the way, and at my very first reception in his office many years ago, I was struck with his extraordinary warmth and kindliness. Surgeon General Jennings followed General Heaton, then General Robert Bernstein, now Commanding Officer of the Walter Reed Medical Center; Col. Oscar Adams, Retired, with whom we worked for so many years on so many projects; those who followed Col. Adams, Col. Hal Heady, Ret., Col. Bob Haas, Ret., and Col. Charlie Christ and all the staff of the OTSE. In the Chief's Office of the Corps of Engineers, Tom Payne and Jim Allred. In the Navy, Admiral Corradi, retired Chief of the Bureau of Yards and Docks, and Admiral Riggs, Chief, Bureau of Medicine.

All of these D.C. people were and are friends. Around a table there is but one common purpose, to produce the best result.

In the Baltimore District on Walter Reed we have worked with four consecutive District Chiefs: Col's. Love, Prentiss, McGarry and Withers; at the civilian level, a very particular friend is Carl Schletzer who in April 1977 retired as Chief, Structures Branch.

When I think of Letterman, the late General Jack Schwartz, Commanding Officer of Letterman General Hospital and his Chief Executive, Col. James Mackin will be forever remembered as personal friends.

At the Twelfth Naval District in San Bruno, Retired Capt. John Burkey, Commanding Officer, remains the closest of friends as does Retired Admiral Michael Marshall, Chief of Naval Facilities who in the earlier days was Commander Marshall at San Bruno.

The list has grown in recent years. John, as well as others in the office, could now add many, and our relationships and friendships continue.

101. SHRINERS HOSPITAL FOR CRIPPLED CHILDREN, (Joshua Freiwald). View from lower street. One story and two stories, due to sloping site, both of same full configuration. Out-patient facilities and ancillary services on lower floor. Warm and non-institutional, characteristic of its purpose and spirit, and respectful to its residential neighbors.

102. SHRINERS HOSPITAL FOR CRIPPLED CHILDREN, San Francisco, 1967 (Joshua Freiwald). View from upper street.

SHRINERS HOSPITAL FOR CRIPPLED CHILDREN

In 1965 the late Messrs. Albert Jacobs and Wm. Coffman, the originator of the East-West Shrine Game, first talked with me about the Shrine Hospital For Crippled Children in San Francisco.

After a thorough study, it was determined that the best interests could only be attained by the construction of a new hospital rather than remodeling of the existing hospital, the fourth unit of the charitable Shriners Hospitals, now numbering twenty-two units.

The closure of one street plus the abutting property thereto provides a park-like site, 980 feet in length and 240 feet in depth, with an abundance of open green and planting.

The new hospital is clothed with an exterior of non-institutional design, employing tile roofs, brick walls, arches and traditional elements in contemporary forms. The residential neighbors are respected by its scale and low profile, and it is compatible with the original structure, now used for the administrative purposes of the Islam Temple of the Shrine.

It is a thoroughly functional facility. More particularly, it is "home" for long periods for most patients, and they, regardless of race, creed or color are here due to "the world's greatest and most satisfying philanthropy."

The foregoing description is more detailed than others herein. Perhaps so, but I am attempting to describe the feelings that prevailed when designing the facility. See the children, understand their faith and their emotions; see the doctors, nurses, technicians and volunteers whose skills, care and love are dedicated so completely to the healing and the happiness of the children. Without sharing or understanding this, how could one create a place that nurtures these qualities? The understanding and appreciation of unique conditions was particularly required here; and inside and outside, I think a beautiful "home" was created, not an institution.

Miss Clara Wallace, Administrator of the Hospital, epitomizes the qualities referred to. Working with her, the Building Committee of Albert Jacobs, Ira Coburn and Howard McKinley and the local and national Boards of Governors was rewarding. Our greatest reward is in the knowledge that our efforts have aided in the care of and love for the children.

I drive by the Hospital quite often because it is on 19th Avenue, a cross town artery with the highest auto traffic count in San Francisco, with signals well synchronized. I drive as slowly as I dare, taking in the 1,000 – foot frontage, hospital well set back, with grounds kept immaculately. I like very much what I see.

103. SHRINERS HOSPITAL FOR CRIPPLED CHILDREN, (Joshua Freiwald). Main Entrance, upper street.

104. PINE TERRACE APARTMENTS, San Francisco, 1964 (Joshua Freiwald). Pine Terrace is a 164 unit condominium apartment building located on Nob Hill. Exterior walls are of exposed aggregate concrete panels.

105. CALIFORNIA DEPARTMENT OF MOTOR VEHICLES, Sacramento, 1953 (Joshua Freiwald). The utilitarian purpose of the building indicated a direct, uncluttered statement, which was accomplished with clean horizontal overhangs for sun protection, and infill window wall panels.

OTHER WORK AND FRIENDS

Obviously, much work of the office has not been discussed in detail and much not even mentioned. No jobs are unimportant but some understandably come more sharply to mind than others. Perhaps those involving continuity seem uppermost. Certainly we take pride in this but we think of all of our work with pleasure.

Why, for example, have I not spoken of our work for the Crocker National Bank? I better do so, for my brother Bill was Executive Vice-President of the Crocker Anglo National Bank until his retirement in the early '60s, a Director then, and for many years after! William W. Crocker was a very personal friend of Tim but in Tim's time there was no bank work to be done; in the '50s and '60s we did a good deal of Crocker Bank work including the remodeling of the exterior of No. One Montgomery and all the interior floors thereof.

This building, erected very soon after the 1906 earthquake, is notable, since Willis Polk of Daniel Burnham's office in Chicago designed it. He and/or Daniel Burnham did many of the Renaissance buildings as the City rebuilt. Above its classic granite base, the limestone veneered upper stories and cornice were spalling badly and were in fact dangerous. It had to be removed and replaced. A lightweight glazed terra cotta was used after thorough structural analysis of the building by the late Walter Steilberg, structural engineer.

106. CROCKER NATIONAL BANK, San Francisco, (Gabriel Moulin). Number One Montgomery Street, San Francisco Headquarters, before renovation. Designed by Willis Polk and erected in 1907.

107. CROCKER NATIONAL BANK, (Gabriel Moulin). After renovation. In the refacing, necessitated by the falling of spalled fragments, due respect was given to the original design, and there was no attempt to "modernize" the character.

108. CROCKER NATIONAL BANK, 1968 (Joshua Freiwald,. A small branch building on Geary Street.

109. CROCKER NATIONAL BANK, Oakland, 1950 (Gabriel Moulin). Main Branch, Oakland, California.

However, the ceramic veneer facing leaves much to be desired. A thin granite veneer, also found to be structurally feasible on the existing frame, had been selected and a full size mock-up, constructed at the quarry, had been approved; then word came down that due to very influential pressure upon the bank, ceramic veneer had to be used as the facing material!

Other work for the then Crocker Anglo or Crocker Citizens included branch buildings in San Francisco, Oakland and Monterey.

Emmett G. Solomon, former President of the Bank, now Director of the Crocker National Corporation and Chairman of the Executive Committee of the Crocker National Bank was a Deacon of the Church of St. Matthew in San Mateo. English Country Gothic, designed by Willis Polk and built soon after the quake had destroyed the original building, it was a beautiful church, but inadequate for the greatly increased congregation. Emmett Solomon and his committee decided something had to be done and we were commissioned.

All possible concepts were explored, none seemingly really satisfactory. The extraordinarily beautiful southwest facade with its large stained glass window was set well back from El Camino Real. Here let me quote in part from Dorothy F. Regnery's book *An Enduring Heritage*, Stanford Univerity Press, 1976, wherein she describes and illustrates historic buildings of the San Francisco peninsula. This is an excerpt from her piece on the Church of St. Matthew.

". . . By 1950 the congregation of the parish had far exceeded the building's capacity, but the parishioners were unwilling to consider extensions that would endanger the perfection of their church's design. In 1956, Milton T. Pflueger came up with a novel solution. He literally cut the church in half and inched the front end of the nave a full 30 feet to the south. The project was so beautifully engineered that not a single window was broken nor was the plaster cracked. The new section inserted in the space increased the seating to accommodate an additional 160 people. . . ."

So it is that at times the Architect does not only create. With a thought and the assistance of Huber and Knapik, our structural engineers, and the artistry (I can think of no other word) of Tim O'Sullivan, the "house-mover" with whom I had had experience for many years, the moving and the insertion of two fifteen-foot bays, identical with the original nave bays, were the means to a most satisfying end.

THE GUATEMALA STORY

Two special friends, Ed Cahill and Jack Younger, flew Ed's plane to Mexico and Central America at least once yearly for many years. They obviously loved the countries and the people. About five or six years ago Jack visited the small village of Nuevo Progreso, about one hundred and seventy miles north of Guatemala City and there met the Reverend Father Cayetano Bertoldo, who had built a small Mission and School. The Father mentioned his dream of some day adding a small clinic to treat the many ills of the 2,000 villagers and perhaps 20,000 natives in nearby villages and coffee plantations.

On Jack's return to San Francisco, he was quite determined to find this need satisfied. Friends responded, knowing the facility would be built by the villagers under Padre Bertoldo's supervision , as had the Mission. Jack asked me if I would design it (not another Walter Reed, but one from which he knew I, too, would receive a special satisfaction).

The thought of a "small clinic" soon grew in accord with the generous responses, and today in this mission there is a thirty bed hospital, and a clinic which treats more than 10,000 out-patients yearly; all possible because of the labor of the natives, who cut down trees, hand sawed them into lumber, broke rocks into aggregate for concrete, and carried one hundred pound sacks of cement on each shoulder.

One of Jack's earliest listeners was Dr. Harold Marquis, retired San Francisco internist. He and his wife Mary, a registered nurse, went to the Mission before the hospital was completed, spent several years training native girls in nursing care, physical and mental therapy and giving of their own knowledge and skill to their patients. Their devotion inspired others, and there are now other doctors (particularly from San Francisco) who are dedicated to the care of these natives in a far distant country.

The story of the Hospitale de la Familie again demonstrates the compassion and generosity of individual Americans for the poor and needy people of the world. It also demonstrates how the devoted efforts of individuals, in this case Reverend Father Bertoldo, Mr. Jack Younger and Dr. Harold Marquis, can make dreams come true.

I am reminded of this story by the Diploma, "Honor al Merito," to Arquitecto Milton T. Pflueger which hangs in the office.

A sequel which is not to be forgotten: A year or

so ago, John flew to Guatemala City with Jack Younger. They were met by an old friend of our family, Mr. Gustavo Stahl who lives in Guatemala. Gus had never met John, and his first words were, "My gosh, I never thought I would see Tim again!"

John not only resembles his Uncle Tim, he has many of his most remarkable attributes.

* * * * *

Early in these recollections, the Olympic Club was referred to; along with THE FAMILY and the Bohemian Club, it afforded Tim times of great pleasure. It may be that I have written so little of the Olympic Club because it was there he had just had his nightly swim moments before his untimely death, and that evening with its tragic end remains the greatest shock of all.

But with time, how sweet are the other memories, before and after. John came into the Junior section at the age of nine, and his pleasure and interest have never waned; I think he will go on with the intra-mural basketball for many more years. His golf, however, has been greatly curtailed by the demands of business—too bad, because as all fathers, I believe he could have been pretty good—and those purses! We think often of the three or four "pitching" holes he constructed in our steep back yard in 1950. He was 13, and a half acre lot (a rarity in San Francisco) did provide space for a very few tiny greens; but Lakeside, with its two great courses, was and is becoming more so a bit too much. I speak now very definitely for myself.

We have a "fearsome fore-some" and this is how it began. Wally Sheehan and I became Directors of the Club in 1957, serving the usual three years. Bob Walsh and Andy Glover came on the Board in 1958 and 1959. Friends before, our friendship grew ever stronger, and the golf games have been going on, the quality of our games having no effect on the fun we have, on the course and otherwise.

The Olympic Club has had a long and most interesting history. William F. Humphrey, president from 1907 to 1953 (the Club was originated in 1860), was by far its most forward looking champion, guiding and strengthening it with strong will and purpose. In 1953, when by special election the by-laws were amended limiting the terms of presidents and directors, many members were deeply saddened; the new rules, perhaps providing a more democratic process, nevertheless marked the end of Mr. Humphrey's many years of unselfish, tireless effort and devotion. The change might well have been made without a disquieting note, which was not the case.

I was glad that for some years prior to that time I came to know and value the friendship of Bill Humphrey and his directors, and had been working with them on our plans for the interior alterations to the downtown Clubhouse; although the working drawings were not completed until 1954, and construction in 1955. Although no longer "in office," Bill was proud of yet another accomplishment which instigated greater use and pleasure for the membership.

These reminiscences of the Olympic Club were triggered in part by my Guatemala Story, which saw a dream come true. The Olympic Club, specifically the downtown property, recalls a dream which to this time at least has not come true.

For nearly as long as memory serves, development of the property has been discussed. Bill Humphrey had my brother Tim (and Arthur Brown, Jr. also), develop concepts for the use of the corner of Post and Mason Streets many, many years ago. The corner, a fifty vara by fifty vara piece, has been retained by the Club by means of short term leases to tenants, in order that full benefit might eventually accrue to the Club. (Parenthetically, the vara is an early Spanish measure of length, 2.75 feet, and is no longer commonly used. Our City blocks, north of Market Street, are 100 vara x 150 vara, 275 feet by 412.5 feet—just a passing thought.) Development then has been a continuing subject, and proposals abundant.

It was in the early '60s that President Al Cleary and his Board appointed a "Forward Planning Committee," a committee of five (to serve for five years), its purpose to review and bring forth forward thinking to assure not only continued well-being but progressive action—a broad assignment indeed.

As a member of that committee, I thought more and more of the downtown property and its possibilities, going so far as to envision acquisition of the abutting property to the rear of the Clubhouse on Sutter Street, which was (and still is) poorly utilized. Here could be built a new Club, expanded to every conceivable need, and one which would meet all new code requirements. The present Club, having been built in 1911, of course does not, and making it so, or physically adding thereto, which would mandate code conformance, would be extremely difficult and costly.

While building the new facility, the use of the present clubhouse could continue without disturbance, an important factor. Upon completion of the new facility, the old clubhouse would be demolished and the entire property on Post Street, from the Bohemian Club to Mason Street, over three hundred feet, and one hundred thirty seven and a half feet in depth, would be developed to its best use under the most favorable considerations to the Club. A great opportunity was lost when the dream was not diligently pursued. Development of some kind will have to take place, but I am afraid it will fall far short of the grand dream I had. Had Bill Humphrey been still at the helm, who knows?

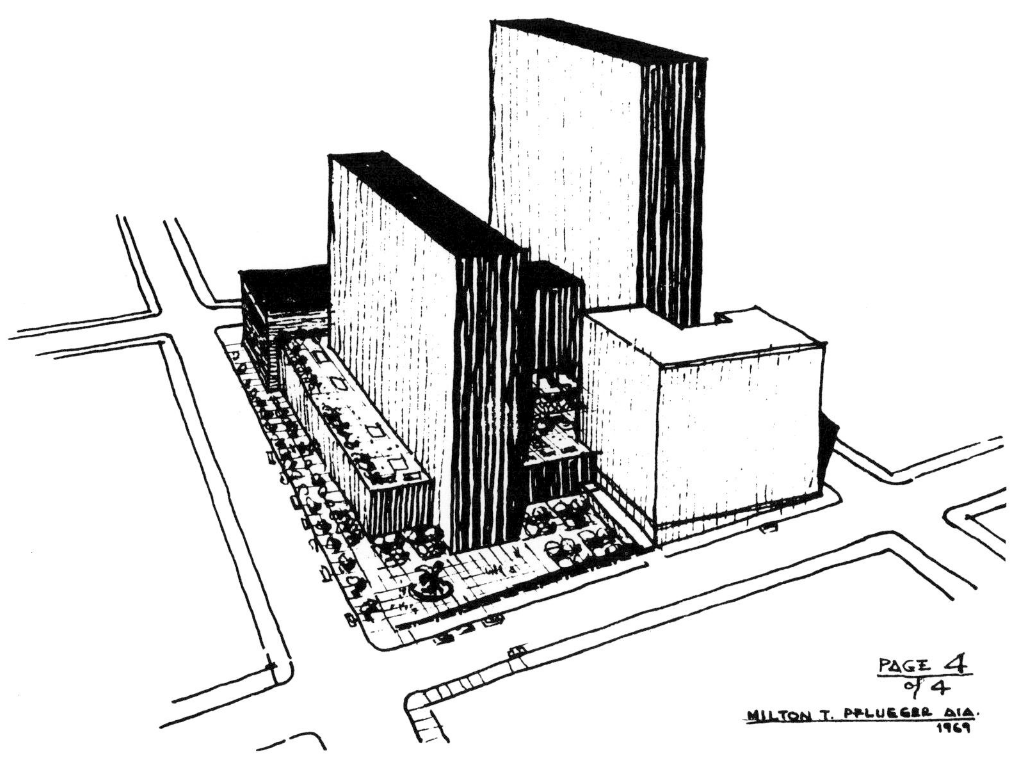

110. THE DREAM, 1969 (Milton Pflueger).

111 & 112. SAN JOSE STATE UNIVERSITY LIBRARY, San Jose, 1980 (Robert Van Noy). These photographs of the south facade show the mirrored undersides of the solar spandrels. The reflections in the mirrors add an interesting liveliness to the facade.

CHANGING OF THE GUARD

Certainly, if I were now actively and personally involved in all the details of the office, there would not be enough time for the writing of these reflections.

Years ago the elder brother led the younger, who as father then led the son; in recent years and henceforth, the son leads the father. That seems very personal and it over-simplifies past, present and future. It omits so much, so very many associates and friends who make it all real.

Our clients, old and new, have made it abundantly clear that the firm, under the strong leadership of John, is providing the highest quality of personalized professional service. It must be so, otherwise we could not speak of continuing and new clients.

We are working for all of our "old" clients—and they say we have never had finer relationships—and with new clients such as San Jose State University, where a new library building may well be the first large building in the U.S. designed to heat and cool itself with natural passive systems, and where Angelo Centani, the University Planning Director, has offered the observation that no previous presentations, on any work, have been as professional as those by John.

He has worked with and made many friends in a Corps of Engineers project, one in which I might have declined to become involved: the Corte Madera Creek project, in which with Royston, Hanamoto, Beck and Abbey, the landscape architects, a solution to flood control involved humanization and nature's enhancement, not concrete canals.

113. SAN JOSE STATE UNIVERSITY LIBRARY, 1980 (Robert Van Noy) The building is sited on a large landscaped square which is mainly bordered by smaller buildings constructed decades ago. Strict compatibility in character and scale, (if in any manner achievable) would have been false. This south facade, with tilted solar panels, sloping mirrored soffits (adding solar efficiency), tile roof recalls and other design features, fits well in place.

These thoughts will not be restrained and regardless of the father-son relationship, or perhaps very much because of it, I very thankfully try to put them in words. Planted in the early years of this century, the tree flourishes, because its roots are strong.

Having succumbed to the temptation of philosophizing, and since all of this has been for self-pleasure, why not express one more thought.

The appreciation of the beautifully spoken or written word, the sound of music and laughter, nature in all its wonder, love of life and fellow man, art in all its forms: this appreciation is a requisite in a full man, whatever his work. It follows then that it is presumptuous to say that appreciation is or must be in the possession of one type of man, or one engaged in a particular field of endeavor. Yet I presume to think that this appreciation and sensitivity would well accompany the technological skill in the making of an architect.

If we perform our technical and emotional tasks with skill, preserve and enhance our natural and man-made environment, then we will contribute to the advance of man.

There is no end to this story. It will be continued, and hopefully the future episodes will be increasingly eventful.

October 1977

114. BATMALE HALL, CITY COLLEGE OF SAN FRANCISCO, San Francisco, 1979 (Robert Van Noy). The dramatic structural system and lower level circulation streets reveal themselves on the east side of the facility. As these floors are stepped into the hillside, major protected outdoor spaces are available on each level and the curved ground and walkway patterns enclose and soften the strong structural concept of the facility.

AFTERTHOUGHTS I, 1977

Having read what was written, I realize how many happenings and thoughts have been overlooked. Most particularly, I am aware of how sketchy and lacking in depth are my words about Tim and how matter-of-factly work and events of our lives are dismissed. Certainly more time, at least a little research to spur my memory, would have been so much better. That this was written without a "plan," without careful forethought, at broken, odd moments, now is very evident. A certain sense of urgency prevailed in setting down these recollections. That is my excuse.

Thoughts continue to surface—with a phone call, a piece of mail, a dream and for many other reasons. Should a few be added? They, too, will be unplanned and sketchy.

* * * * *

Tim's concern regarding the ecletic, stylistic approach so prevalent in his earliest years, his search for change and timely solutions to new challenges, led him inevitably to increasing inquisitiveness and creative capacity. This credo, coupled with his professional integrity and idealism, is the heritage of the firm. It is cherished, and inculcated in those who followed.

* * * * *

Rooms are not rooms, ceilings ceilings, nor walls walls.

A bit more of the Top of the Mark as a point. When I started studies of room elevations, windows were great and large but the studies were still "wall elevations." No, no, said Tim, no walls. I caught on and before too long was in tune. If we practically could have eliminated elevators and toilets, in order to have one unbroken sky space, we would have! The hotel boiler stack, piping and flues—these also would have to remain, but we "wrapped" them as closely as possible, in their own free configuration, minimizing bulk, maximizing sight lines. All arrises and corners were eliminated throughout, helping to create a spatial atmosphere, not a room.

Do you feel the "fun" and excitement that was always there working with Tim—lessons never to be forgotten?

* * * * *

I look at early exterior studies of our Shrine Hospital. Yes, well proportioned and more than acceptable design. But where is the spark, the joy of something special, the beauty of particular appropriateness? It came, this time not quickly or intuitively, but with study, patience and perseverance; also a lesson not forgotten.

* * * * *

On ceilings. In the Castro Theater, recently named a "landmark" in our city, which was opened in early 1922 and which Tim did well before the age of 30. Here an ornate Oriental canopy of decorative plaster hangs above the theater auditorium. In the late '20s, the metal "fins" created a cover in the great spaces of the San Francisco Stock Exchange Trading Room and in the Paramount Theater, a national historic monument. Or the USO "Stage Canteen," where a gaily decorated cloth canopy was used. This, in World War II, was where our servicemen were entertained and found their relaxation. Judges, executives, entertainers and people of all stations gave their time to men and women in the service. It was a place for fun and forgetting for a moment. How we loved its purpose and atmosphere, particularly Tim, who gave so much to its creation and management.

Or the Oriental tapestry that inspired the lobby ceiling of the Telephone Building. Or the great swaths of hanging cloth in the Arts in Action space of the '39-'40 Exposition, filtering and obscuring the strong sunlight through the existing skylights.

* * * * *

In the early '30s we thought, why run toilet partition stiles to the floor, thus creating floor cleaning difficulties? We first made them of wood (same as the doors) and hung them from the ceiling. Soon this became standard, even with marble and metal stiles, by all manufacturers; but our first were custom made and detailed.

The first flush lobby elevator fronts, floor to ceiling, were made for the Pacific Telephone & Telegraph Headquarters. Elevator manufacturers did not make door hangers to permit this, but Tim insisted, and Otis reengineered and this became standard.

The decorative fin ceilings of the Stock Exchange Trading Room and the Auditorium and Lobby of the Paramount Theater obscuring the back lighting were "firsts" and were later developed into the "egg crate" features of many standard lighting fixtures.

The door stops of door frames always went to the floor until the early 1940s. We asked ourselves why, because this created small, hard to clean corners. Although it cost more, we terminated the stops at base height, and we detailed flush stainless steel bases for the frames in the Department of Surgery at the Herbert C. Moffitt Teaching Hospital. All hollow metal door frame stops (particularly in hospitals) now terminate at base height.

At I. Magnin's in San Francisco we fully detailed an electrified window washing rail and scaffold at the roof in collaboration with Lamson Company. (There were none at the time.) The cost was prohibitive. Skyscrapers (which I concede, Magnin's is not) could not now live without them.

Our consultants in every discipline are also urged to advance innovative ideas. At the War Memorial Gymnasium at the University of San Francisco, Tommy Thompson designed the then longest prestressed barrel vaults known, and our full height exterior precast panels at Harney Science Center were a "first." Our research and study in all fields of energy has been a must, as it should be in every structure.

I could go on with stories of this nature, as I think of imagination, concepts and details which fulfill practical needs and delight the eye.

* * * * *

It is not implied that we are unique. It can be said, however, that over many years we have been asked why we have developed special details or designs and have never given consideration to patenting. The answer has been that these are our services and we had our satisfaction thereby.

There recently was one change from this position. On the Fish Roundabout at the Academy of Sciences, we designed view window mullions and frames that are unique. Heretofore the water pressure on the glass of an aquarium (which is transmitted to the surrounding metal frame) has always been resisted by frame connections on the wet or tank side. In our detail the connections are on the dry or viewer's side; they can be readily adjusted while the tank is full; the detail also eliminated maintenance problems which are prevalent when connections are on the wet side. The Roundabout itself with its 100,000 gallons of sea water, 3" thick Plexiglas view windows and other features is quite unique in itself. We felt the frame design so superior that it was worthy of a patent and one was obtained.

* * * * *

The world, becoming ever smaller, grows in its complexity. The age of technology is forcing our lives into the control of organizations, corporations, associations, groups large and small. Yet, now as always, the individual is the keystone. Every advance is still sparked in its beginning by an individual. The fulfillment of an idea, concept, if there is fulfillment, usually requires the greatest collaboration on the part of others, but this is secondary. The genesis, the origin, will ever be in the mind and heart of one alone.

* * * * *

In any field of creativity, how difficult it must be to be a critic; upon what elements do you judge—in your own being, other beings, or perhaps in the being of the creator?

I recently received a letter, received certainly by all local architects, asking opinions regarding a nationally known architect's concept for the new store building on the site of an existing historical landmark building (The City of Paris). The letter was most persuasive, and indicated grievous concern regarding the concept. Much has been published regarding the matter.

Almost concurrently, a University architectural history student called our office and asked how was it that Arthur Brown was referred to as the architect of the original building when she herself had seen blueprints with "James R. Miller, Architect" (Tim's employer and later partner). I'm afraid that I was too short, saying perhaps, "Sorry, but that was all before my time." I had forgotten that our tracings (J.R. Miller's) and a very few Bakewell & Brown prints of the same time, 1908-1909, had been loaned from our files to the Foundation for San Francisco's Architectural Heritage some years ago.

I had also forgotten that these were "completion" drawings and that neither Bakewell & Brown nor James R. Miller was the architect of the original building but of the building "completion," including the Rotunda which has been so highly treasured. J.R.'s drawings and specifications were very complete considering the circa.

All of this culminated in a dream I later had. I saw what I could only describe as a small "Thumbs Down" trophy mounted on a base upon which I most vividly read the inscription, "We (who, the A.I.A.?) hereby fine (who, the Architect?) for failing to find the morning to see."

Every Architect knows the significance of these words. We struggle and study through the "night," awaiting to find "the morning to see," that moment when the solution seems clear, when doubts and alternatives are erased. Surely our work is not for us alone and therefore we are subject to "fines" and criticisms. Those who judge, however, are also on the stand; their judgement should result only from careful consideration.

I am reminded again of the Stanford Advisory Board of Architects. How careful we have been never to "design by committee," attempting with utmost objectivity to understand the Architect's rationale, never knowingly "fining" for his failure to find the morning to see, but rather offering viewpoints which may have been overlooked.

Is this straddling the fence, fearful of yes or no, equivocal? I hope not, liking to think that I suggest criticism, praise and judgement are most serious.

* * * *

"Less is more." "Small is beautiful." "Progress is our most important product." Shoot the Moon-Mars-Venus and so on. Nuclear Fission or Fusion. "Friends of the Earth." Life or no Life. Mostly extremes, all or nothing. Where is the common ground? Where is our golden mean and moderation?

What does this have to do with architecture? A great deal, in my belief. Architects, more than most professionals, are trained to think logically. Does this prohibit innovation and forward thinking? Not at all. If logic and reason accompany the innovation, order and not chaos will result.

Am I contradictory? Great leaps have been made throughout the history of mankind, and this will always be. These are attributable in most part to the genius of one man or woman alone. Those who see and think far ahead are as necessary as our daily bread. Then come the followers, those who question, those who believe, and here is the crux. Let us question or let us believe, but give us the ability and intellect to do so with reason.

* * * * *

At sometime after Tim's death, Hervey Clark, a San Francisco Architect, phoned to tell me that the area Chapter of the American Institute of Architects had proposed Tim for Fellowship in the Institute, but had been regretfully informed that a posthumous award would be contrary to rules.

Although a member since my eligibility, I had no great interest in the Institute and merely thanked Hervey for the information, recollecting inwardly that some years before, upon receiving a singular honor, Tim had facetiously remarked "Well, it's about time!"

A short time passed before I realized a sense of resentment that Tim had been proposed at such an inauspicious time, rather than years before when such a proposal would have reflected recognition not only on the receiver, but on the Chapter as well.

* * * * *

Consider only some highlights within the broad scope of his work in the 1920 and 1930 decades: The Telephone Building, 450 Sutter, San Francisco Stock Exchange, Paramount Theater, San Francisco Bay Bridge, the Federal Building and other work at the Golden Gate International Exposition, the Top of the Mark, Union Square Plaza and Garage, the fostering and integrating of the Fine Arts into his architecture. This had all been accomplished years before his death, and speaks not at all of his work in the 1940s and that which was in progress at his death in late 1946.

In my early travels, in visits with architects across our land, the exceptional regard held for Tim was clearly evident.

Chapter initiative was required before the National Board could bestow Fellowship. It is no wonder that as time passed it became increasingly difficult for me to understand that a sudden premature death was at last the cause for Chapter action. It was kind of Hervey to express the regret, but I confess the phone call instigated a sequence of thoughts which remain to this day.

* * * * *

Everything that is done, everything that happens, is somewhere, related (and most things are). There they are, hopefully to be remembered, to be used or not. You pick and choose, accept or reject, but they are there. One thing leads to another, the mind races on, sometimes too quickly for reflection.

Julius Girod, John McLaren's protege and successor, landscaped the Golden Gate International Exposition beautifully. He landscaped Union Square for us, personally selecting the sixteen large yews and the palms for the Square from the grounds of the Exposition.

My brother Otto, the surgeon, was in the Army Air Corps in World War II. One of his Stations was Blythe, the southernmost desert of California, a hot, arid, plantless Air Base, to put it mildly.

What in the world is the connection? Well, Tim in his usual concern speaks with Julius. Together, one finding the materials, the other supplying the funds, they transport trees, and other plant materials to the Base, where the personnel gleefully plant and nurture them, a project which meets with qualified success, due to nature's adversity.

* * * * *

Not all things are rational, nor envisioned. After the completion of our Graduate School of Business at Stanford, Wally Sterling and I were standing far across the Oval, at the far end of the Quad facade. Wally said, "Milt, this must have been designed just so. Look at that roof behind the School." The central portion of the School is a story higher than its two wings. But even above the tile roof of our central wing, there behind it loomed the tile roof of the stage loft of the Memorial Auditorium (done long before by Arthur Brown), seemingly a crowning glory.

I wish I could have agreed. Certainly we did not wish, there was no need, that our central roof was high or higher than the stage loft roof, but just as certainly we had not envisioned the view and exact juxtaposition from that particular vantage point. I am sure most architects have had the same thrill. Conversely, I'm sure many have felt disappointment in that which they saw after their project was completed.

* * * * *

Every year at least, Tim flew to the East, renewing friendships and seeing new things. When you flew, it was in a small mail plane, with a pilot and a single passenger, or at most two. While I was still at Bakewell & Brown, therefore 1926 or 1927, Tim and a fellow passenger were on one of these trips. The pilot had missed the pass and crashed into the snow topped Rockies. They were not found for well over two days.

Brother Bill and I flew to Elko in Nevada, not that we could help, but to be near the search. The fliers finally spotted the plane; packers found all three miraculously unharmed, and brought them out.

The relevance is this. Just as Tim visited his architect friends around the country, so did his friends see him here on their visits. The personal exchanges far surpassed reading of each other's work. When I came to Tim's office, I remember many such meetings; quite frequently I went along to dinner and a night out. Those occasions were most informative and rewarding.

* * * * *

Having only older brothers, it comes to me that perhaps the friendships I recollect most fondly are with men older than I, not that much older, but enough so that too many are no longer here. Yet this is not entirely true. Time and time again I am grateful that John and I are together, not only in work but in friendship and company. His friends are mine and mine his. Yet John remembers well those occasions when he was a little fellow and Tim would come by in his Cad convertible, top down, and take him for a spin. Our span covers some years and we have something not given to all.

Names of hundreds of friends and colleagues who have been close over the years of our professional life should have been included in this volume. For these omissions I am truly regretful.

Over-sentimental, over-sensitive, I must be. Tears come too readily, with happiness and sadness. We can be tough though. This has often been said and is very true. What a paradox. John says that is the German in us.

* * * * *

I have strayed it seems from architects and architecture. But how does one separate work from life and family? It is all one, isn't it? If so, what of the distaff side of the Milton Pflueger family?

Sister Emily Marie, of the Sisters of the Holy Names, not only more than helped in the design of the College of the Holy Names, she watched every driven nail and every yard of concrete. As we ended a business conference in our office one day, and just upon leaving, Sister asked me, "How is it Mr. Pflueger, that you found such a lovely and kind person, and persuaded her to be your wife?" Now we hadn't been talking of Gen, whom Sister Emily had met several times, and though flustered, I recovered to answer, "Well, Sister, I think I've always had good taste, and I was very, very lucky." I would not care to change my answer, knowing what hit me fifty years ago, married close to forty-five years, and having this love every moment.

Ann, our daugther, almost five years younger than her brother John, is a treasure, having inherited all her mother's goodness and loveliness.

With John's three boys and Ann's two boys (yes, no sisters!), who knows? Could there be another architect?

Afterthoughts are endless. So many things still to remember, not said or written.

But it seems an appropriate time to end, today, Friday, the thirtieth day of December 1977. I will go on remembering, thinking, working, but why not close the book temporarily.

December 1977

AFTERTHOUGHTS II, 1980

Having finished the "Afterthoughts I" in December 1977, it seemed a good time to put this all aside. Without thought of dissemination, it seemed the continuation should be left to John, if he in the future would be so inclined. However, almost three years have now elapsed and now in 1980 a persuasive feeling urges further notes of these latter years, particularly for one reason.

In this year 1980, after more than 60 continuous years at the 580 Market Street location, the office has moved. We are now on Tenth Street, below Mission in what was originally a public bath house built by James Lick in 1886. The name James Lick evokes many recollections—a personal one interests me. Along with much more, he gave to the City the Francis Scott Key Memorial Statue which was located in front of the Academy of Sciences in Golden Gate Park. When we did Cowell Hall at the Academy, the statue was dismantled, stored, then re-located at its present location, the easterly end of the Music Concourse. Now we are linked to an earlier facet of the legendary James Lick.

The structure of our new quarters has been reinforced, the brick walls sandblasted; new skylighting, steel trusses and timbered roof, everything exposed including the new mechanical and electrical installations. Some new partitions, new and old furnishings, and new equipment are all combined to provide unusual and most attractive quarters. A far cry from 580 Market.

115. BATHAUS, PFLUEGER OFFICE, San Francisco, 1980 (isometric drawing: Pflueger Architects).

BATHAUS, PFLUEGER OFFICE

1980 (Robert Van Noy)

116. The mezzanine of the original building, before renovation.

117. A Chinese Laundry had occupied a portion of the building for forty years prior to our occupancy. This is the Main Laundry Room before renovation.

118. The boiler room of the Bathaus, shown here, was converted to the main conference room of the Pflueger Office. See Illustration 159 Page 116.

119. One end of the mezzanine space, after renovation into Administrative Offices.

120. The old main floor Laundry Room after renovation. It is now the primary Drafting Room.

121. The Reception Area of the Pflueger Office, after renovation.

122. CALIFORNIA FARM BUREAU FEDERATION HEADQUARTERS, Sacramento, 1981 (Robert Van Noy). View from Exposition Boulevard. Visitor parking near main entrance. Staff parking in the basement and contiguous depressed area, over which future expansion is planned.

The office relocation forced a tedious yet reassuring task in certain aspects, one being the verification of my recollections of events long past. No tricks were played by my memory. In our long history it seems that nothing was thrown away. Personal records, letters, clippings, magazines, special editions, photos, certificates of awards—national and international, all was found in one place or another. I have gone over all and found that the failing in my writing was not in misstatements but in so many omissions. So while memory did not trick me, much of interest was not revealed. In the very beginning of my recollections I said there would be no research, which was just as well. Had I at that time, my task would have seemed insurmountable.

In these last several months of revelation, I have re-lived the years, and this without reading the daily diaries which Tim began in 1919 and which I have continued to this time. While not journals (no time for that), the notes on meetings, calls, reminders, names, events would be too much to cope with.

My little story is so inadequate and had I now the patience, it could be told so much more appropriately. It will be left as is, without additions or rewriting. A bit about the last two-three years will be told and this will be even briefer than before.

This is unjust to John, upon whom now rest all responsibilities, and also to those who with him have made strides which only the strong and most able can make. Unfortunately, my will seems unequal to a lengthy tale.

The Walter Reed Army Medical Center Hospital in Washington, D.C., dedicated in September, 1977, while still in the finishing stages of construction is, of course, fully operational. This facility, 1.2 million square feet, 1280 beds, involving technological and design advances of the highest degree, is a milestone in the history of our office. The 134 million dollar building (construction cost dollars of 1972) fulfills the high expectations envisioned when we were commissioned in 1968.

The Library at San Jose State University is in construction. As we move on with ever increasing energy costs, the value of its solar energy system multiplies.

At San Francisco Community College, the building which was called Cloud East during design and construction, was dedicated as Batmale Hall in 1978.

In December 1979, with only finishing touches remaining, the Headquarters Office Building for the California Farm Bureau Federation in Sacramento was dedicated. In just two years this large steel frame, 2-story building (with underground garage) was designed and constructed. It has many innovative features, all well calculated and designed to meet strict client and community criteria.

Both the pre-selection of a most able general contractor and a fast-track schedule resulted in savings of many months in overall time and more than a few hundred thousand dollars. For some years the Owens-Corning Company has conducted an annual national competition for excellence in

123. CALIFORNIA FARM BUREAU FEDERATION HEADQUARTERS, 1981 (Robert Van Noy). Daylighting above interior light well.

124. CALIFORNIA FARM BUREAU FEDERATION HEADQUARTERS, (Robert Van Noy). Landscaped berms cover parking and protect building interior.

125. CALIFORNIA FARM BUREAU HEADQUARTERS, (Robert Van Noy). Courtyard dining area with berms to the left and deep shadows created by overhangs to the right.

126. CALIFORNIA FARM BUREAU HEADQUARTERS, (Robert Van Noy). Solar panels and skylights over light wells.

127. CONLAN HALL, CITY COLLEGE OF SAN FRANCISCO, San Francisco, CA, 1968 (Joshua Freiwald). The Educational Services Building is named Conlan Hall to honor Louis G. Conlan, the President of the College for 21 years, 1949 to 1971. Its Entrance Portico, here shown, faces the sloping green, the forefront of the College, and recalls the portico of the Science Building, the first and most dominant building on campus.

128. BATMALE HALL, CITY COLLEGE OF SAN FRANCISCO, San Francisco, 1979 (Robert Van Noy). The dramatic structural system, deep reveals, walkways and office plaza are all visible from the lower views.

architecture with combined energy conservation design of innovation and practicality. In 1979 the prize award in the commercial building category was presented to Pflueger Architects for the California Farm Bureau Federation Headquarters Building. The Federation Board and Mr. Fred Heringer, President, exercised great foresight years ago in purchasing a large site, the major portion of which is still to be developed in accord with a Master Plan.

Schematics have been made for a new Ingleside Hospital in Rosemeade, for which the Certificate of Need is forthcoming. Mr. W.H. "Bud" Newell, President/CEO of the Center, and the Board are enthusiastic and valued clientele. The Program for the Center, developed in close cooperation by our office and the Center achieved an award for Program Development and Conceptual Design.

Plans are near completion for several commercial developments in neighbor counties of the Bay Area as part of a vigorous program by the Larry Lyons Construction Company of San Mateo. Other developments are in consideration.

Work for long time clients such as the University of San Francisco, Stanford and the College of the Holy Names continues. It is with great pride that it is well nigh impossible to think of a client who, once having started with us, has then forgotten and foregone our relationships.

For well over two years intensive and continuous effort has been expended on what is certainly one of the exciting projects in our office. It is in Reno, Nevada. A Cultural Center with the Fine Arts and Performing Arts is always challenging; in conjunction with a new headquarters of a large statewide Bank it is even more so.

Here we speak of the Sierra Arts Foundation and the Nevada National Bank, the combination of facilities into one complex.

Culture is a significant sign of progress in our civilization. Ever increasingly there has been evidence of the promotion of cultural appreciation on the part of private enterprise. Institutions are recognizing the mutual benefits which evolve with active contribution to cultural advancement, culture being the need and right of all society, a necessary balance to materialistic gain. It is exciting to participate in the development of a project which will clearly show that Reno, with its Sierra Arts Foundation and its new headquarters of the Nevada National Bank, is in the mainstream of forward planning. All of this is not easy. The leaders have shown great perseverance and devotion.

George Aker, President of the Bank, and the Board of Directors, the Board of the Foundation with President Thomas Wilson and hard working Vice President Carol Mousel, the City Administration, the many Benefactors—to these are due all credit for a grand vision. I think with great fondness of my very personal Reno friends of so many years; particularly Les Gray who carries on with unfailing support the aims of his late wife, a devoted Founder of the Sierra Arts.

With friends such as these, and also I prefer to think because of our professional record, it is not altogether strange that we were selected from among so many to do this project. I think of Glenbrook on the Nevada side of Lake Tahoe where the Bliss family gave us so many, many summers of delight, and our friends there, year after year. The Shaws, Marrins, Marks, Hoovers, Lissers, Crafts, Hunters, Huntingtons, Pollacks—every name evokes a picture of parents, children and grandchildren returning year after year to enjoy the beauty of the Lake and the Sierras. Joe Moniz, the golf pro and his lovely Mary with whom we would party, even a bit too much at times. Of course, brother Bill and Charlotte who never missed for more than fifty consecutive years and who introduced us to Glenbrook's wonders.

So it is that Nevada is much more than only geographically close, it is a second home. For John, this is now literally true, for his work there requires great devotion and gives much more than ordinary satisfaction. He is to be envied and I must count myself among the envious.

John has just executed with the Corps of Engineers a contract for the design of Administrative Facilities as required for the MX Missile System. Obviously, since I write of this, this design contract is not yet determined but the scope of the first phase of Administration is well defined, with provision for additional phases. To have been selected for such an assignment is gratifying, if I may understate it. The commitment to the System has been made. Our work will soon begin.

It was some months ago that my notes on the Reno, Nevada Project and the nostalgic Glenbrook memories were made. Feeling near the end of my recollections, I put this aside. Now, in mid-December 1980, I have just noted the Missile Project. The two are poles apart, and there seems an incongruity in extolling the pleasure of working on a business - culture job and immediately thereafter a job relating to a military missile system.

129. *NEVADA NATIONAL BANK HEADQUARTERS, Reno, 1982 (Robert Van Noy). Main banking room with photo murals of the Great Basin.*

130. *NEVADA NATIONAL BANK HEADQUARTERS (Robert Van Noy). The greenhouse containing bank offices and conference areas.*

131. *NEVADA NATIONAL BANK HEADQUARTERS, (Robert Van Noy). Early winter morning at the main building entrance.*

132. *NEVADA NATIONAL BANK HEADQUARTERS, (Robert Van Noy). The west facade with the deep sun-shaded reveals.*

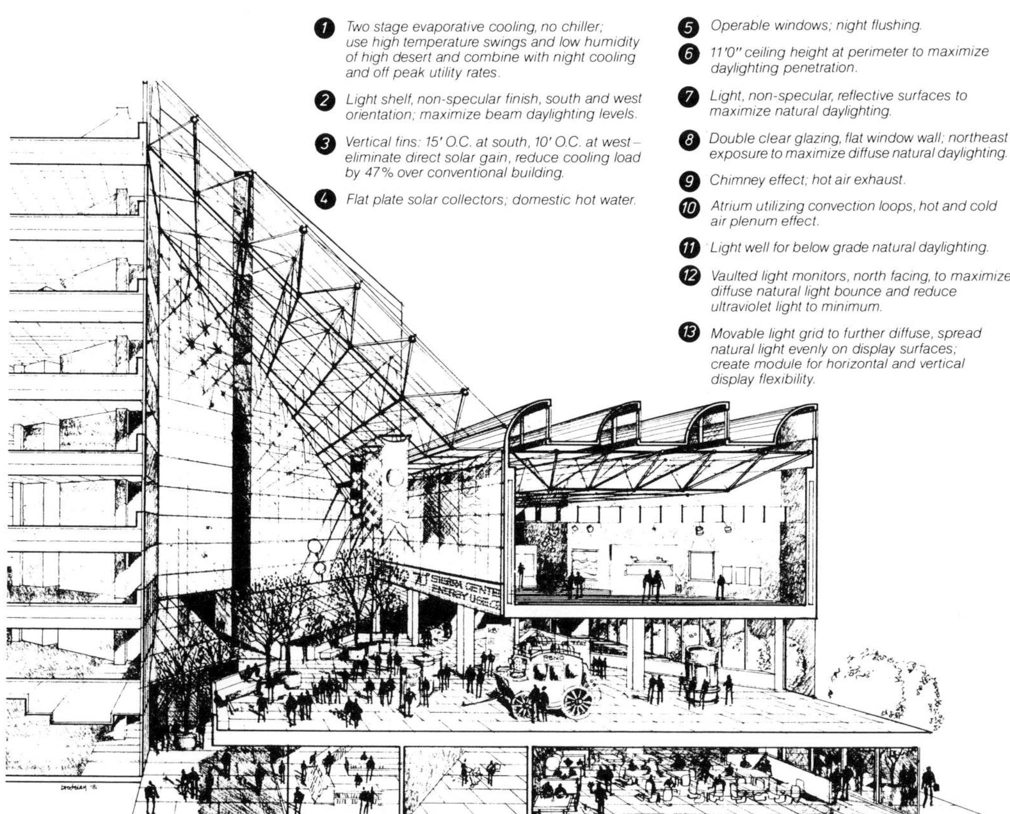

133. SIERRA ARTS FOUNDATION/NEVADA NATIONAL BANK HEADQUARTERS, Reno, 1982 (rendering: David Brodsley). The Atrium of the total complex, including the Bank and the facilities for the Arts Foundation. The text describes the energy system of the complex.

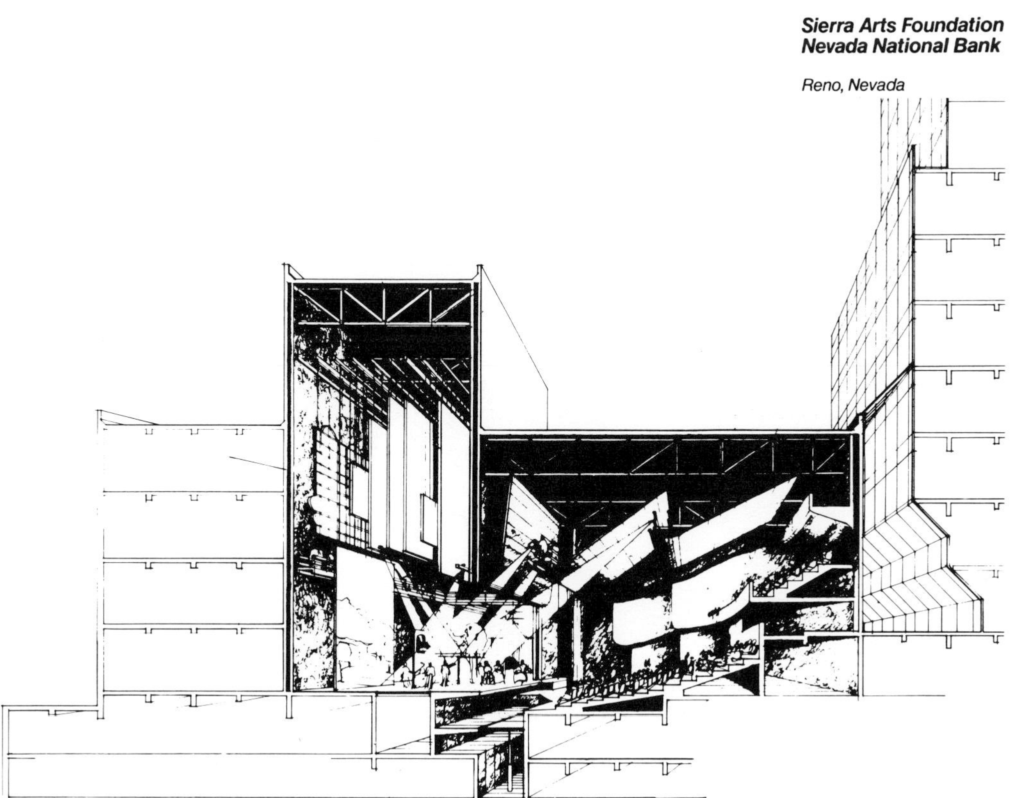

134. SIERRA ARTS FOUNDATION/NEVADA NATIONAL BANK HEADQUARTERS, (rendering: David Brodsley). Main theater of Performing Arts Center.

One could well ask, is it possible economically to proceed in both areas, or must one be sacrificed? At this time, and at this point of decision-making in our country, the answer seems that we really can't have one without the other. Our way of life—our culture—our freedom—all were attained at great cost; if we are to retain them, then military strength, also at great cost, is necessary. The accomplishment will be most difficult, but in this transition phase of our governmental leadership, the confidence that it can and must be done has never been stronger.

Plans must be made, and this is at once both figuratively and literally true. The course must be set.

The fate of Pflueger Architects loses its all-importance as we contemplate the problems of our times. However, we serve best by supporting a strong, righteous leadership and by continuing in our personal endeavors to the very highest degree.

We will remember the good and bad times, and fervently hope that we may be permitted to continue the kind of practice we feel so well qualified for.

To conclude and affirm my deep convictions. In my brother Tim, I had the best teacher. There was from the beginning of his career a greatness which found and created the highest expressions of his art. Fifteen years younger, I carried on, and was more than mindful of the example set. Then the transition to John, who has accepted his role and more than fulfulled my expectations.

Now, in December 1980, my ever diminishing role gives both regret and supreme confidence—regret that one cannot continue with all vigor, but confidence in that the best is yet to come.

We all have answers, true or false, simple or complex, for the mysteries and desires of our lives, the why and wherefore. The answers all vary; how dismal if life and answers were all alike.

I also have some in the afternoon of my life, when ambition is lessened and when I thankfully leave decisions to the young and more capable.

Now my answers are emotional and from the heart, rather than intellectual and from the brain, and they are merged into one. I have been given the life-long love of a courageous soul, a beautiful soul of goodness and understanding. For me, this answer far outshines all others.

December 1980

Milton and John

AND NOW, 1981

Now we are three. When I first started my recollections with the list of Pflueger brothers I said, "Paul (1891-)." On April 9, 1981, our brother Paul passed away.

Now, as we age, it would be unreal to not know, or be surprised at the certainties. It also becomes very clear, however, that the certainty and inevitableness does not still the feeling of emptiness.

I wrote then that I wished for time and ability to tell of the accomplishments of all my brothers and of their love and influence on the baby brother. I still do, but although time is there, the ability to set my thoughts in order and give full, thankful appreciation is beyond me.

Paul would not have his family, his children, grandchildren, great-grandchildren, nor his brothers grieve, and we do not. As the youngest brother, I pay reverance to the eldest for it was he throughout a long lifetime, who set the good examples for all.

Of that generation, the children of August and Ottilie Pflueger, there now survive three. The family and generations after are many. May they flourish and continue to receive God's Blessing.

Paul would say "God Bless All," thinking of all mankind without reservation, and so must we all say, and believe it.

Of we three, Bill, Ott and Milt, Bill is by far the most active, and a truly remarkable man. An abdominal aneurysm of the aorta, necessitating the removal of the "y" and the implant of a plastic substitute, kept him down for what I consider only a relatively short time. Paul had exactly the same condition quite a few years ago, then I also about seven years ago. We have come to believe in the "physical basis of heredity," but due to remarkable skill, fine care and good genes, we have done well. I must recall a personal incident and its subsequent effect upon my general outlook.

On one post-operative night in the cardiovascular care unit, my eyes opened, and sitting there at bedside, gazing intently into my eyes was my surgeon, Dr. Frank Gerbode. I was sane enough to say, "Why Doctor!" What are you doing here in the middle of the night?" His reply, "Well, I have a good friend here in the Hospital, and I had to see how he was coming along."

A good friend, indeed. It was not until several days later that I knew I was the "good friend" and fully realized just how great and kind this man is. He had also operated on my brother Paul; and, of course, Paul and the thousands of other patients of Dr. Gerbode have been his "good friends." I think of this very often; and just a week or two ago, a notice comes that the Frank Gerbode Chair for Research and Development will assure the continuity of the Medical Research Foundation which bears his name and which has been under his direction for more than two decades.

With every passing day, I thank God for Dr. James W. Good, for it is through his care and knowledge that Gen is well and at my side, more than a few years after hope was all but gone.

Men such as these, and they are there in every field of endeavor, by their individual unselfish devotion to ideals and convictions will prevail. The "Ascent of Man," as Jacob Bronowski so beautifully depicted, will not be stilled. We were not created and put upon this earth with extinction of humanity as an end.

Two weeks ago, for the first time since 1976, I was at the Family Farm. Otto, Lloyd (Paul's son) and I spent the Midsummer weekend at our Camp 31, of which camp John is now also a member. Tim was the first, certainly no less than sixty years ago, and now four Pfluegers are in it, with tolerance and kindness on the part of our camp members. Just when our campmates went to bed on Friday night, Lloyd and I cannot remember; but the two of us were alone and stood at the bar talking until dawn broke at 5:30, at which time, almost reluctantly, we called it off and got to bed.

The point is that we talked of Pfluegers the entire time, interspersed you may be sure with tears and laughter. I am somewhat concerned at just what this is a sign of, but the concern will not stop my confession to a long night of thankful recollections. "Pflueger Architects" seems off-stage momentarily; family has taken over, but without apology.

My life still offers things for me to do. There is a very fine, comfortable place for me in the office and John keeps me advised, even asking for suggestions which, of course, pleases me greatly. The past is always there, with renderings, photos, paintings, and other memorabilia.

The present is there with both old friends and new, rolls of drawings, models, and all that one finds in a busy architect's office. Were I to dwell only upon the problems of our unrestful world, the future might seem bleak, and I would wonder what lies in store for our children and their children. I choose to be counted among those who have faith in righteousness and I hopefully will continue to have a part in the struggle for its survival. Each of us must do that which we can best do.

There is no end to an "unfinished" story, but the end of my writing is long overdue. I do so with a very simple bar chart which indicates the chronological record of Pflueger Architect Principals.

It would be a pleasure to amplify the chart to include all related factors such as Staff, Clients, High Points, etc., etc. We are all aware of computer capability, micro-photography and other technological means by which, with proper input, a full and complete "picture" might be produced.

That would be a most interesting excercise, and perhaps my story should have started and developed with this in mind. The upper bar is the source. I trust my words have revealed the love and admiration I feel. Any evaluation of the middle bar is not for me to say, nor is the length of its extention. The lower bar is well on its way.

I have spoken with pride of our continuity. The "Splicing Periods" denoting the time frame of togetherness are very relevant. One could not have premeditated this. Would only that the upper bar had gone on, and that the first Splicing Period had been much longer. I thank God the second one, though very much diminishing in its import, goes on.

Carry on, John.

July 1981

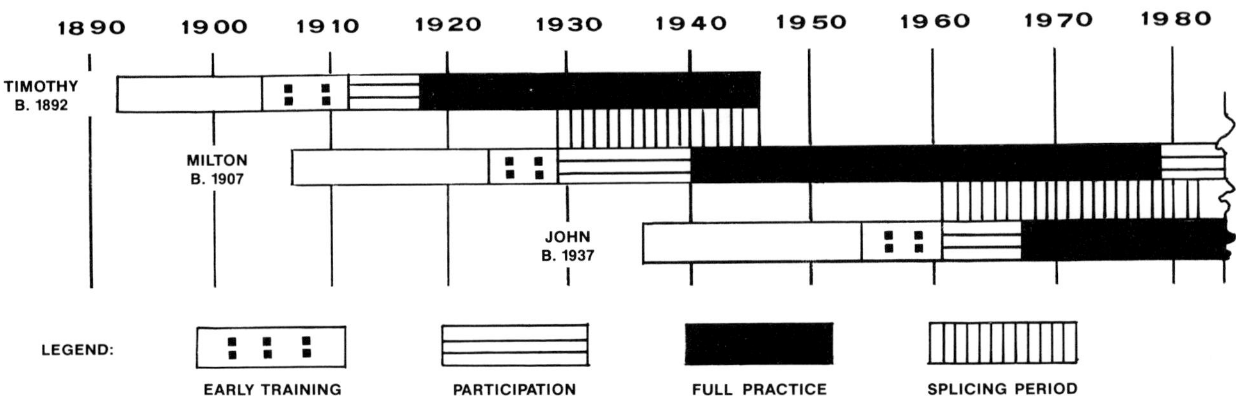

THE COLOR INSERTION ON THE
FOLLOWING PAGES REMINDS US
OF THE BEAUTY AND JOY THAT COLOR
BRINGS TO OUR LIVES AND TO THE
WORKS OF ARCHITECTURE

PARAMOUNT THEATER

Oakland, 1931

135

136

137

138

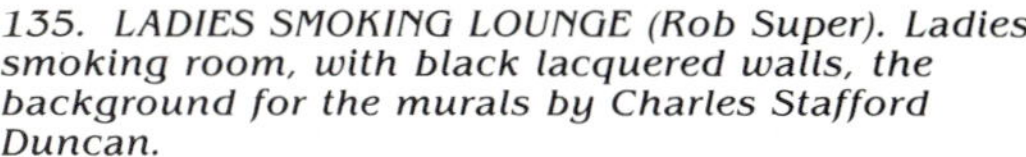

135. LADIES SMOKING LOUNGE (Rob Super). Ladies smoking room, with black lacquered walls, the background for the murals by Charles Stafford Duncan.

136. THE ORGAN GRILLE (Roger Minick). From the stage proscenium; the organ grille, sculptured walls, and light column on the right (light columns frame the sides of the proscenium).

137. GRAND LOBBY (Rob Super). A view of the Grand Lobby from the mezzanine foyer. Above the entrance doors is the etched glass Fountain of Light. No walls, no ceiling— all is glass and open metal fins, back-lighted—imaginative creation.

138. THEATER CEILING (Rob Super). The theater ceiling from the stage. One should not call it a ceiling; it is a sky with colored light filtering through forest leaves or lacy clouds—whatever the imagination conjures.

139. THEATER AUDITORIUM (Roger Minick). Susan Harper, a.k.a. Susannah Harris Stone, authored "The Oakland Paramount" in 1981, with photography by Roger Minick. Here, in this photo, you are at a side aisle in the 15th row of the orchestra; the curving balcony front is directly above you and the balcony soffit light fixtures are glowing; the stage curtain and valance are in place, framed by the vertical Light Column; there is the organ grille and the sculptured wall reaching to the 60-foot high ceiling, then bending out to frame the leafy metal-finned ceiling, aglow with its filtered colored light.

For me, it is again Opening Night, December 16, 1931; all 3500 seats with people in their "finest," musicians in the pit are playing, the Fanchon & Marco Beauties are dancing on stage; at my side is my beauty, Gen, (I would have to court for yet another 2 years); the entire audience is gazing in awesome delight at one detail, then at another in this grand space.

140. RICHMOND CIVIC CENTER, Richmond, 1949-1951 (Phil Fein). The Civic Auditorium. Red Roman-size brick is the basic exterior facing material on all buildings.

141. COLLEGE OF THE HOLY NAMES, Oakland, 1958 (Joshua Freiwald). The Chapel and Bell Tower counterpoint the low horizontal composition.

142. SAN FRANCISCO STOCK EXCHANGE, San Francisco, 1930 (Charles H. Hays). The Stair Hall, connecting the Lounge and Dining floors, features the Diego Rivera fresco.

143. CIRQUE ROOM, FAIRMONT HOTEL, San Francisco, 1983 (Photograph courtesy of the Fairmont Hotel). This room was recently restored to exactly the way it was when first completed in 1935 and called the CIRCUS LOUNGE. It is now called the CIRQUE. The circus murals are the work of Helen Bruton, assisted by Esther and Margaret, Helen's sisters.

142

143

144. UNIVERSITY OF SAN FRANCISCO, GLEESON LIBRARY, San Francisco, 1951 (Joshua Freiwald). The Richard Gleeson Library was the first building constructed in the new development era.

145. GOLDEN GATE INTERNATIONAL EXPOSITION, San Francisco, 1939 (Gabriel Moulin). Night lighting was, of course, a feature. Here, Arthur Brown, Jr.'s Tower of Sun dominates.

146

147

146. GRADUATE SCHOOL OF BUSINESS, 1966 (Joshua Freiwald). A Student Lounge and intimate outdoor Place feature the south side of the building. (The north and west facades relate to the Oval and Quad.)

147. STANFORD TENNIS FACILITY (Robert Van Noy). Far removed from campus influence, it was economically imprudent, and deemed unnecessary to design in the traditional Stanford vocabulary.

LELAND STANFORD JUNIOR UNIVERSITY

Stanford, 1957-1983

148. CENTER FOR BIOLOGICAL SCIENCES, 1967, (Joshua Freiwald). The Teaching Wing from the higher Research Wing of the complex. The Hoover Tower and the Quad are in the background.

149. STANFORD TENNIS FACILITY, 1983 (Robert Van Noy). Multimedia space affords teaching, lounge and display opportunities.

150. DINKELSPIEL MEMORIAL AUDITORIUM, 1957 (Joshua Freiwald). Ceiling detail in Auditorium.

151 & 152. CALIFORNIA ACADEMY OF SCIENCES, WATTIS HALL OF MAN, San Francisco, 1973 (Rob Super, Peter Gerba). The Hall of Anthropology provides maximum flexibility for exhibits. A hanging gridiron system and a mirror bend at the intersection of wall and ceiling, creating an illusion of endless space. A close view reveals that only one half of an exhibit is actual, the other half being a mirror reflection.

151

152

CALIFORNIA ACADEMY OF SCIENCES

San Francisco, 1973

153

154

153 & 154. CALIFORNIA ACADEMY OF SCIENCES, MEYER FISH ROUNDABOUT, STEINHART AQUARIUM, 1973 (Rob Super). The 100,000 gallon, doughnut-shaped tank, the first of its kind in the United States, is the only kind of tank in which schooling ocean fishes can be kept. One enters the viewing space by a ramp from the floor below and is then surrounded by the 10 foot high tank. Water jets create a current against which the fishes swim. The 3 inch thick plexiglass view windows are mounted in a unique, patented system, one which utilizes the water pressure to aid in sealing the tank and also minimizes maintenance.

155. SHRINERS HOSPITAL FOR CRIPPLED CHILDREN, San Francisco, 1967 (Joshua Freiwald). Main Entrance from forecourt.

156. SILAS B. HAYES ARMY HOSPITAL, Ft. Ord, 1968 (Joshua Freiwald). A side-rear view of the sloping site with the block of in-patient floors atop service floors; patients are afforded a long-range panoramic view of the magnificent countryside.

157. LETTERMAN GENERAL HOSPITAL, Presidio, San Francisco, 1967, (Joshua Freiwald). The Main Entrance facade with in-patient block; showing only one story of the flanking wings, (which have roof-top gardens). On this side the in-patient rooms overlook the Presidio; on the three other sides San Francisco Bay and the Golden Gate.

158. WALTER REED GENERAL HOSPITAL, Washington D.C., 1977 (Peter Xiques). Under this on-grade plaza with its two-level entrance drives is the parking structure. Here the building is five stories high, with the three upper in-patient floors cantilevered beyond the lower floors. The sloping horizontal spandrels provide sunshade, also fresh air intake to the mechanical system floors which occur between all floors of the building.

159. BATHAUS, PFLUEGER OFFICE, San Francisco, 1980 (Robert Van Noy). The original James Lick Bathaus had a sunken boiler room. It is now the main Conference Room for the office.

160. SAN JOSE STATE UNIVERSITY LIBRARY, San Jose, 1980 (Roberto LaMantia). On the sun-oriented facade, the solar panels are unabashedly featured, characterizing the mandate of energy efficiency.

161. ORCHARD PROFESSIONAL OFFICE BUILDING, Vacaville, 1983 (Robert Van Noy). The cedar-faced building complements its predominant residential environment.

162. BATMALE HALL, CITY COLLEGE OF SAN FRANCISCO, San Francisco, 1979 (Robert Van Noy). On the downside of the steep site, the structural system is clearly revealed, and the circulation streets lead to protected outdoor spaces.

163. BATMALE HALL, CITY COLLEGE OF SAN FRANCISCO (Robert Van Noy). From a main campus mall on the high side of the site, a bridge leads to a rooftop plaza and building entrance. The plaza, overlooking the cityscape, features integrated sculpture and seating by Jacques Overhoff.

164. CENTRE POINT PLAZA, Fremont, 1983 (Robert Van Noy). At the office building complex; Greenhouse at sunset.

165. CENTRE POINT PLAZA (Robert Van Noy). East and west walls have minimal openings, reducing climate impact.

166. CALIFORNIA FARM BUREAU FEDERATION HEADQUARTERS, Sacramento, 1981 (Robert Van Noy). The reception desk against a backdrop of Robert Campbell photo murals representing the primary contribution of each county to the farming industry of California.

167. CALIFORNIA FARM BUREAU FEDERATION HEADQUARTERS (Robert Van Noy). Overview toward main entrance from Exposition Boulevard, a main artery.

NEVADA NATIONAL BANK HEADQUARTERS

Reno, 1982

168. (Bob Sexton). Column and ceiling detail in Banking Room; a fusion of light and illusion.

169. (Robert Van Noy). A skyward view at the vertex of the two facades.

170. (Robert Van Noy). Lobby and Information Center of the building.

171. (Robert Van Noy). Here, we are looking south on Virginia Street, the main street in Reno. The west facade (with the sunny exposure) has sun screens and light-reflecting shelves, while the converging facade (north-east exposure) has an open window-wall treatment. The design of the building thus responds directly to both solar orientation and maximum daylight considerations.

JOHN PFLUEGER's CONTINUUM

My father and everyone who contributed to the book thought that it would be appropriate for me to trace my history in the firm, and express my thoughts about the present time and the position of the firm after over three quarters of a century as The Pflueger Architects. Our firm has remained committed to the traditions that my father and Timothy established. The integration of the Arts with Architecture is one of the most important traditions, and certainly our work has repeatedly expressed this concept. Another principle upon which we have based our work is the conviction that the design and form of a building would be based on the natural and/or built environment. We have continued to expand and experiment so that the original principles have taken on new dimensions, and in addition we have committed ourselves to a third principle—that of integrating energy conservation into the basic criteria of a building's programming and design. First though, I'll trace my history and, as the years pass, these traditions and principles will constantly reveal themselves.

BACKGROUND

I entered the office in 1961, after completing five years at Stanford University, a short stint in the Air Force, and part time work for the architectural firms of Paul Huston in Palo Alto, and Ted Vierra in Honolulu. In my early years as the boss's son I often felt I was supposed to be "the leader of new directions," but at the same time I felt I was simply "irresponsible," and only of "marginal talent" and perhaps not up to the whole endeavor. It wasn't until 1966, when I obtained my license and won an award in the Santa Rosa City Hall Design Competition, that I began to feel that I could contribute to the firm. My participation expanded as I became involved in our work at Stanford University's Graduate School of Business and Center for Biological Sciences, and developed close ties with our established clients at the California Academy of Sciences, University of San Francisco, College of the Holy Names, and City College of San Francisco.

EARLY YEARS

In 1968, the Joint Venture, which had completed 3 major military hospitals, submitted a proposal for the Walter Reed Hospital, plaza, and underground garage in Washington D.C. We had some reservations because we thought the project would take too much of our resources for too long a time. Also, a project three thousand miles away was contrary to our desire to remain a local firm. Conversely, the job became a milestone for the firm and a tremendous opportunity to culminate our military hospital work. After a long and involved national selection process we were awarded the job.

While the design/production job went full blast, consuming most of my father's time and the firm's resources, I became directly in charge of several projects, including Cowell Hall at the California Academy of Sciences, and the Creative Arts Complex and Cloud East (Batmale Hall) at San Francisco City College as well as the Visual Arts Center, Conlan Hall Union and Smith Hall Addition. Working with Dutch Conlan, Lou Batmale (who used to referee my basketball games), Harry Buttimer, all Presidents of City College, and Vic Vaio and Vic Graff was especially satisfying. These projects reflected the firm's commitment to its three guiding principles; the integration of art and architecture, the blending of a building's design and form with its environment, and energy efficient design.

CALIFORNIA ACADEMY OF SCIENCES AND CITY COLLEGE OF SAN FRANCISCO

Cowell Hall is the entrance to the California Academy of Sciences and the monumental link between the existing classical North American and African Halls. The building's design expression developed with Jim Tuley, Project Architect, was formulated in part through the innovative use of pre-cast concrete technology, and consequently won the national Pre-Cast Concrete Institute Design Award in 1969.

The Creative Arts project at San Francisco City College integrated energy conservation into the building's basic design. To complement the building's solar orientation, the south and west classroom walls were designed with vertical and horizontal shading. The classroom wings are wrapped around the sound isolated broadcasting and T.V. studio. The building is pedestrian-oriented and connected to existing facilities through the use of bridges, platforms and plazas. The building became an extension of the existing Arts Facilities. The project was a 1974 A.I.A. design award winner.

Perhaps, though, the most significant of the three buildings was the Cloud East Building where our efforts were focused even more on energy efficient design and significantly expanded outdoor pedestrian amenities. We placed the building circulation and core space on the south side of the tower and buried three floors and over sixty percent of the building into the east facing hillside. Deep sun shaded openings for the window walls and operable windows were provided. The resulting multi-level, two acre outdoor pedestrian streets and rooftop plazas sloped down the hillside.

Using the City's works-of-art budget, we attempted an unusual integration of art with architecture. In collaboration with sculptor Masatoyo Kishi, a quarter-acre, fiberglass environmental "place" was proposed for the primary rooftop plaza adjacent to the main campus mall. But because the system and the material was untested, the art commission would not approve the design. As a result, Jacques Overhoff, another excellent Bay Area sculptor, was then commissioned to implement the environmental idea of a "place," in concrete. However, due to budget limitations, Overhoff's creation was markedly smaller than Kishi's and therefore more of a "sculpture" than a "place." Nevertheless, the work complements the visual expression of the building.

During 1974, we started working on the California Academy of Sciences Master Plan, Roundabout, Hall of Man, and Entrance Gallery in Golden Gate Park. The project was challenging, not only because it was nestled into a very natural area of the park opposite monumental Cowell Hall and the Band Concourse, but also because of the unique and complex nature of the design requirements. The roundabout concept was to present a view of ocean schooling fish that would be analogous to a scuba diver's view upon submerging.

In order to accomplish our purpose, our Project Architect, Bill Hutcheson, along with the Director of the California Academy of Sciences, George Lindsay, went to Japan to study the only other two roundabouts in the world. Throughout this project, I worked closely with George and Bill, Paul Davies, Frank Hayward, Maury Cox, Jeff Meyer, Steve Craig, and Frank D'Ome, whose contributions were instrumental in the success of the project.

The San Francisco Art Commission enthusiastically endorsed the project when their approval stated: "Architecture and landscape are married into a composition of striking interest and beauty". The long gallery has been advanced to become a feature of outstanding appeal, first, internally and simply as a space,—in which to pause to be refreshed by the excitement of its form and by its partnership with an outdoor planting area of rare horticultural richness of which the space seems to be part,—and second, externally as an architectural and landscape composition of considerable distinction.

STATE OF THE OFFICE

During the 1960s the office was in an enviable position—established clients continued to provide work. I had been fortunate to be exposed to the people and intricacies of many city, state and federal agencies. I especially remember, for instance, the pleasant days reviewing projects with Art Commission members, Ernest Born, Ruth Asawa, Tony Sotomayor, and David Mayes.

In the early 70s, though, several of our clients' expansion projects were completed and competition was increasing tremendously. We needed to broaden our base with new clients, yet remain a medium-sized firm committed to quality and the personal involvement of the principals. Besides the need to find new clients the complexion of the firm was changing in other ways. For more than five years, my father and I had informally functioned as co-principals, but in 1976 the firm officially became a partnership and the name changed to Pflueger Architects.

At this point, with the work completed at the Creative Arts, Cloud East and the Academy of Sciences, the firm seemed ready to take an even more significant step toward the commitment to energy saving design. By dedicating ourselves to this principle, we inevitably committed ourselves to another design criteria that is an integral part of energy saving design, that is, maximizing the natural aspect of building design.

SAN JOSE STATE LIBRARY

One of our major projects of the 70s provided us the chance to demonstrate the innovative ways in which we could create an energy efficient building. In 1975, Angelo Centani of San Jose State University called me and said he didn't really know about the firm, but heard we were the architects for the Stanford Graduate School of

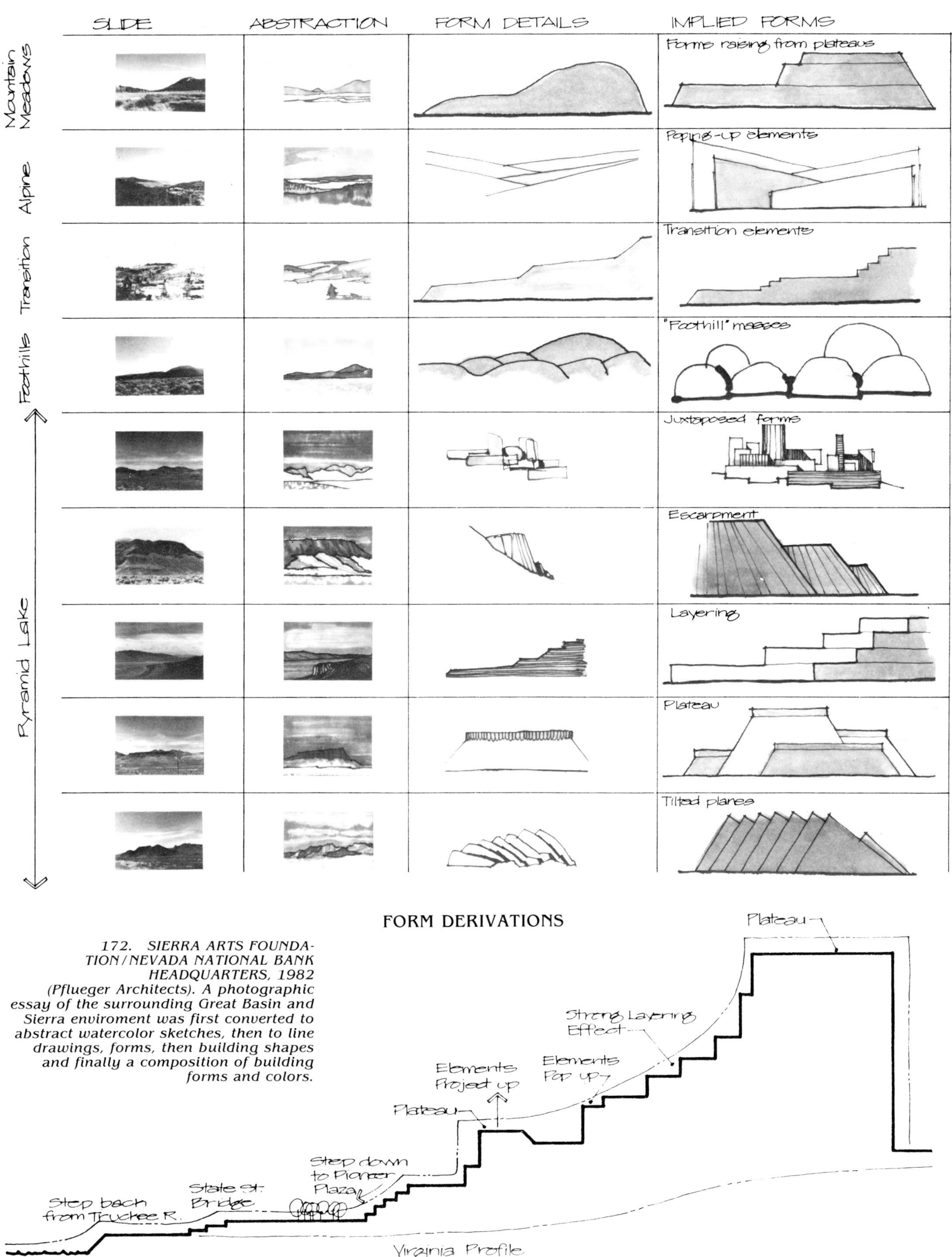

172. SIERRA ARTS FOUNDATION/NEVADA NATIONAL BANK HEADQUARTERS, 1982 (Pflueger Architects). A photographic essay of the surrounding Great Basin and Sierra enviroment was first converted to abstract watercolor sketches, then to line drawings, forms, then building shapes and finally a composition of building forms and colors.

173. SIERRA ARTS FOUNDATION/NEVADA NATIONAL BANK HEADQUARTERS, 1982 (model: Don Bennett). Model of ultimate developments.

174. HEALTH AND RECREATION CENTER, UNIVERSITY OF SAN FRANCISCO, San Francisco, 1983. Photograph of project model.

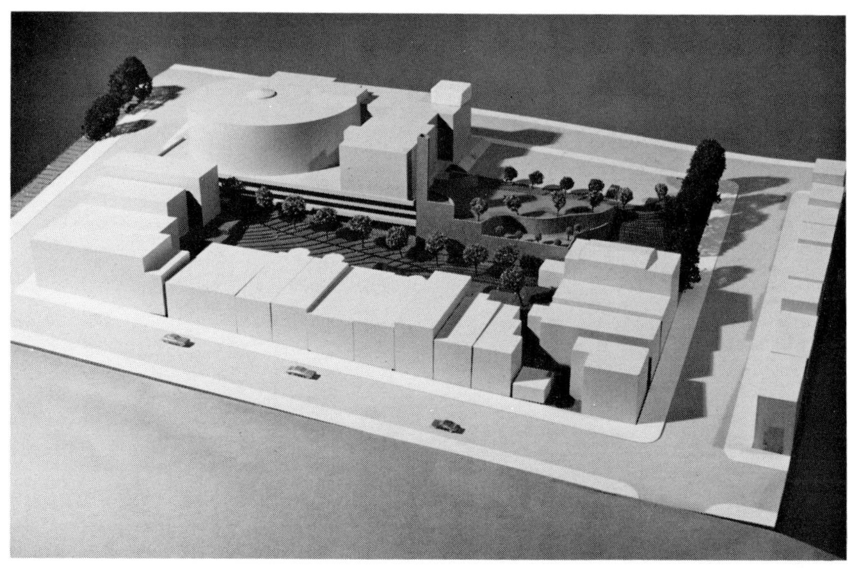

175. COGENERATION FACILITY, UNIVERSITY OF SAN FRANCISCO, 1984 (model: Don Bennett). A nine-megawatt facility built into the hillside and covered with new pedestrian plazas. To its left is Kendrick Hall and the School of Law with its circular library.

176. STANFORD ENVIRONMENTAL SAFETY FACILITY, Stanford, 1984 (model). Three building units surround the processing yard. They contain facilities for handling, testing, processing and disposing of the University waste.

177. STANFORD STADIUM IMPROVEMENTS, STANFORD UNIVERSITY, 1984 (Robert Van Noy). The new Gate 2 Stadium entrance reflects the form and color of the stadium in the backround. Behind the wall are new concession and lavatory facilities.

178. STANFORD TENNIS FACILITY, STANFORD UNIVERSITY, 1983 (Robert Van Noy).

Business. His library job was starting again and he wanted to have the architects of the Stanford Project be his architects. We had never been involved in a State college project and went through a substantial selection process before we were awarded this job.

In our initial orientation and programming work the Chancellor's Office stated we should "heat and cool the building with solar." We responded with our contention that it was not practical or cost effective to cool with solar at the time but to "let us show you what you can do." So we explored and developed many passive and active energy design concepts.

("Passive" or natural energy design simply refers to a method of design that demands a minimal amount of energy. This can be accomplished through mass, insulation, shading, solar orientation, daylighting, free cooling, thermal lag, etc. "Active" systems provide the energy that is needed to operate a building and can be alternative systems such as solar panels or evaporative cooling with no refrigeration, or conventional systems such as boiler produced steam.)

Ultimately, the $11 million, 185,000 square foot building was designed with both passive and active energy systems, although the building primarily relies on its natural, passive design. Each wall of the building is designed to respond to its solar orientation. The basic design concept incorporates concrete mass for thermal storage to obtain a lag in heat and cold transmission, and integrates the collectors into an active south solar wall.

There are small openings on the east and west walls. Natural daylight is maximized on the north and south walls and free night cooling is obtained through the north wall. Because of these passive design features, no energy is needed for over sixty percent of the year. When energy is needed, it comes from an innovative, but simple system of solar hot water panels, water storage, free night cooling and evaporative cooling. We considered rock storage, but quickly realized we would be "building in" substantial problems with subsurface water. We also considered an air system (rather than water) but when combined with a rock system under the building we realized there would be a tremendous need for complex computer controls. Also, an investigation into maintenance problems would result in a situation similar to trying to get inside the pyramids.

A few months after the building was completed a University official said: "The building is a success. The energy systems are simple and unique. The building, though large, fits so well with the older and smaller surrounding campus buildings. The solar wall is nothing like I've seen before. The mirror above tilted downward increases the winter efficiency of the solar panels and reflects the people passing by, which makes the south wall literally alive."

In 1977 we continued our energy efforts with an entry in the State Energy Efficient Office Building Competition which was a recipient of one of the awards.

CORTE MADERA CREEK AND INGLESIDE HOSPITAL

The Corte Madera Creek project in 1976 was of special interest. Certainly one reason was that it was the creek that flooded my house, but also it enabled an architect to be part of an environmental solution usually solved by civil engineers and hydrologists. Our team, headed by Bob Royston's office of superb landscape architects, saved the creek *and* provided flood protection (without a concrete ditch) at a lesser cost.

For several years we have been fortunate to work with Bud Newell and the Ingleside Hospital on their development of new and innovative concepts for Mental Health Care. When interviewed, our lack of extensive mental health facility experience was not a deterrent. Rather, our dedication, enthusiasm, and commitment to working with them in developing a program specifically to meet their needs was the determining factor in our selection. Our program was a 1981 Progressive Architecture Research Award Winner.

CALIFORNIA FARM BUREAU FEDERATION— SIERRA ARTS FOUNDATION

In 1977 we were commissioned to design the California Farm Bureau Federation's headquarters, and Master Plan their 26-acre site in Sacramento. The same ideas employed for the San Jose State University Library were expanded. We integrated solar panels for domestic hot water, water tanks for storage and computer waste heat for space heating. In addition, cool air mass cooling was provided from the underground garage, and a large portion of the building was buried. The end result was a building that uses a minimal amount of energy. An energy audit of the first three years of occupancy has shown a performance that exceeds our projection, and continues to improve annually.

Our accomplishments were acknowledged with one of the 1979 Owens Corning National Design Awards for energy efficient projects, a Department of Energy award, and the 1981 ASHRAE award.

Working with Fred Heringer, his management board, the Farm Bureau Board, and all of the department heads has been particularly rewarding.

In the same year, we were commissioned to design a bank headquarters, a Performing Arts Complex, and a Fine Arts Museum in Reno, collectively known as The Sierra Center. The bank headquarters, now completed, is even more energy-responsive than previous projects. We maximized day lighting—and used no solar panels or water tanks. The air is so dry that the interior environment can be controlled without the active systems we used for the California Farm Bureau and San Jose Library. Passive design is again the key. By using photo cells (not solar cells), foot candles of daylight are measured, the use of flourescent lighting limited, and natural systems are controlled by microprocessors.

With the Sierra Arts Center, we did not limit our approach to the conservation of energy. We also wanted to express the natural surroundings of Reno. In developing the program, one of the first steps was to create a photographic essay of the Great Basin Desert and the foothills and alpine environment of the Sierras. The essay was translated to abstract forms, color, textural impressions and then used to form the basis for the physical expression of the facility.

In both the Farm Bureau and the Sierra Center, we drew heavily on the firm's established tradition of integrating art with architecture, as we had done in earlier projects such as the Cloud East building at City College. In our work as interior designers as well as architects, we constantly have the opportunity to integrate the work of artists with the facility. In the Farm Bureau, the walls contained hand-made quilts and Robert Campbell's stunning photographic essay of the California counties. In the Sierra Center, desert plants, colorful exotic columns, and tremendous photo murals of the surrounding Great Basin were placed in the Nevada National Bank public space. All of this, I must say, reminds me of the Paramount Theater.

The successful energy saving design of the Farm Bureau Building led to our being selected to develop an office support facility for the MX missile system, located in the Nevada desert north of Las Vegas. Energy conservation was a major part of the government criteria and we understood that our success with the Farm Bureau Building had much to do with our selection. In spite of an annual temperature range between 0° and 115°F, we used the dry air, low humidity, high desert elevation, buried buildings and a number of other passive ideas to allow the building to withstand the harsh desert climate while only using 20% of the energy consumed by comparable buildings. The President's decision regarding the MX program in the fall of 1981 stopped the project.

SOME OTHER PLEASURES

In 1978, in a moment of madness on April Fools' day, I bought an option to buy the Santa Rosa Ferryboat. The previous option owners had failed to obtain a permit from the San Francisco Bay Conservation and Development Commission (BCDC) to moor the boat on the bay and use the space for offices. I thought I could succeed and wanted to move our offices to the Ferryboat. After nine months, the BCDC permit was obtained and we placed the Ferryboat on the Register of the National Historic Vessels. Late in 1978 my option for purchase was up and my resources not adequate to purchase the boat.

I was fortunate to find two old friends, Mike McCormac and Dick Bechelli, to join me. Together we exercised the option and bought the boat. My office proceeded with architecture/engineering and interior design. At this point, we realized putting the office on the boat was impossible, and my partners and I sold the boat and project to Lou Coppage from Denver. Now, five years later, the boat is at Pier 3, completed, and fantastic.

Two old friends, Larry Lyons and Tom Molumphy, joined me several years ago and we formed a team providing design, development, financing and construction for several projects. We started with a small shopping center in San Mateo. Then we pursued a resort community in Hawaii, and now we are proceeding with projects in Fremont, Vacaville, Fairfield, and Richmond as well as others. This direction provides increased control of design and the implementation of our energy commitment, and also provides the opportunity for equity participation through development.

THE NEW OFFICE

Late in 1979, when I first saw the 10th Street James Lick Bathaus which had been a Chinese Laundry for forty years, I was captivated. Our office on 580 Market Street was too cramped and after 70 years simply seemed to have outlived its usefulness. The thought of leaving, however, was traumatic. The Bathaus would provide more space and also an opportunity to showcase our talent in preserving and rehabilitating historic structures.

Immediately, we ordered some pizza and beer and invited the whole office to see the building. Was I surprised! Except for a handful of people, they all thought, first with the Ferry Boat, and now

179

180

179 & 180. ORCHARD PROFESSIONAL BUILDING, Vacaville, 1983 (Robert Van Noy). The curved cedar-faced office building blends into its residential environment. The narrow east and west facades are solid to minimize environmental impact on energy consumption while the north and south windows are protected.

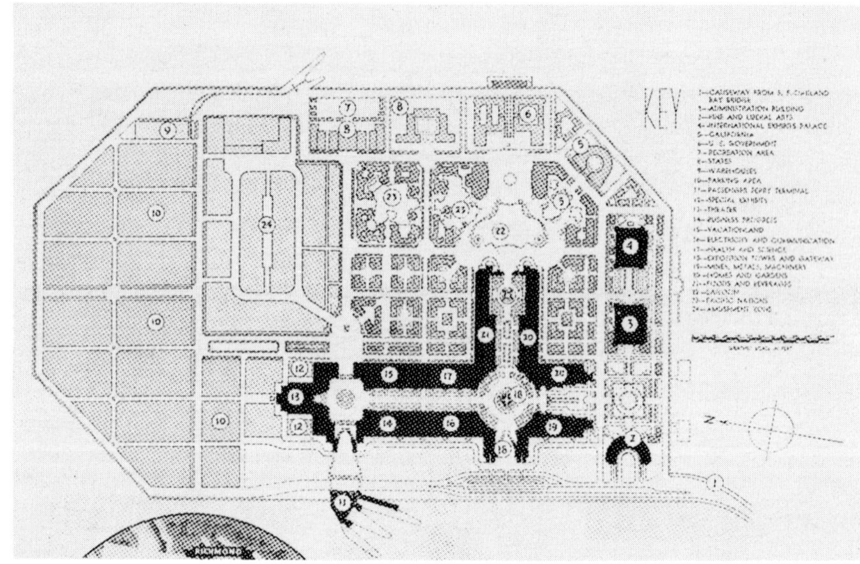

181. TREASURE ISLAND, San Francisco. The original Golden Gate Exposition Master Plan.

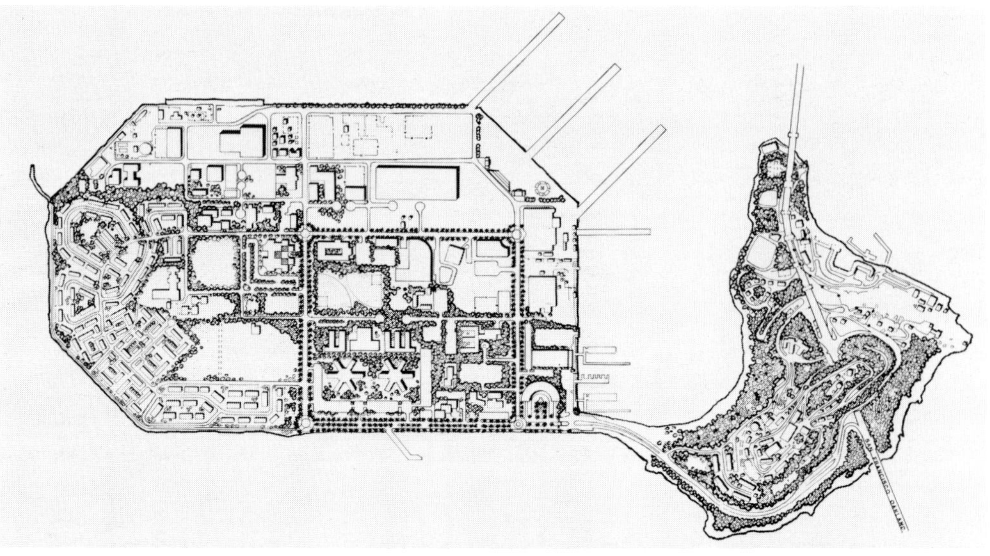

182. TREASURE ISLAND. Master Plan for the Naval Base.

with this building which seemed beyond repair, that I was really hopeless. But in April of 1980, we moved from Market Street to the renovated Bathaus. The job we did in the new quarters has drawn many compliments and brought us new work in restoring old San Francisco buildings.

UPDATE

The recession / depression of 1981- 82 did not miss our office. A significantly reduced work load resulted from the delay or shelving of our three biggest projects and there was simply not enough new work to go around all of the offices in the Bay Area. The beginning of 1983 brought good news and a complete turnaround with an influx of new work. Very significantly this new work is not only completely supportive of our commitment to energy conservation but emanated from our continuing clients.

STANFORD UNIVERSITY

After a decade of occasional work with my alma mater we have made a solid reconnection with the University for whom the office has worked for over 35 years. The Athletic Department and Andy Geiger, Alan Cummings, Dick Gould (both classmates of mine) and Frank Berman asked us to design the first permanent facility for the National Championship Tennis Teams, and facilities to improve the Stadium for the Super Bowl.

The handling of hazardous waste generated by the medical center and research facilities is a sensitive and extremely important issue for all universities, hospitals and industry. The University selected us to design the Environmental Safety Facility where our approach combines the state of the art design with the philosophy of developing an environmental asset rather than liability. This sensitive response in my mind is not unlike our commitment to energy conservation.

UNIVERSITY OF SAN FRANCISCO

Our client for over 50 years has on its own made a total commitment to the reduction of energy use and, as part of this significant thrust, we are working with the University in the design of an environmentally sound and community responsive Cogeneration Facility. To meet community concern the structure will be built into a hillside with the perceptible aspect of the structure limited to terraced, landscaped, pedestrian plazas.

For years Loyola Hall on Stanyan Street (formerly St. Ignatius High School) has been an outmoded, extremely expensive facility to operate. Plans are underway to create an energy self-sufficient sports center which will replace Loyola Hall.

The opportunity to again work closely with Fathers LoSchiavo, Dullea, Callaghan and Ken Goss, Woody Hancock, Al Alessandri, Ron Brill and all the members of the University and neighborhood community is especially satisfying.

NAVY

Over the years our office has enjoyed a continual association with WESTDIV at San Bruno and so we were particularly pleased to be selected to create the Base Exterior Plans and Guidelines for improvements at Mare Island and Treasure Island. Treasure Island was uniquely interesting because of the office's participation in the World's Fair. It seems very interesting that the Navy would welcome our concept of establishing design guidelines for all future improvements at Treasure Island to be based on the World's Fair. Circulation, building guidelines, lighting, landscaping—everything is derived from the Fair.

We couldn't wait to have the opportunity to design the first new structure that would have to meet the guidelines we established. Next thing we know we are selected for the first new project. Little did I expect that this significant, first, new project would be a 300-man Brig!

BANK OF AMERICA AND PG&E

In pursuit of our interest in broadening the ability of consumers to save energy, we asked Bank of America if, although they have incorporated many energy conservation methods in their millions of square feet of buildings, it would be appropriate to develop a uniform system for the management of energy conservation complete with a method of reporting and the establishment of goals and opportunities. They agreed, and PG&E felt such a manual could apply to all their commercial building customers and so joined with Bank of America in commissioning our firm and Flack & Kurtz to develop the manual. The document is unique and can be adapted for use with all types of facilities.

SHRINERS HOSPITAL

One of our projects of which we are so proud and for which so many feelings are attached is the Hospital on 19th Avenue. How pleased we were when given the opportunity to work with Howard McKinley again and all of the people connected with the Hospital in creating their new Spinal Cord Injury Unit.

SUMMARY AND REFLECTIONS

The architectural profession is changing at a pace unrecognizable from year to year. The explosion of technology and the frustration of attempting to correctly or logically predict and plan based on historic, social and economic principles is gone. We cannot expect to see the "good old days" again. It is more important than ever to emphasize simplicity and to remember one's goals, ideals, the identity of the firm, and most importantly, the identity of each individual within the family.

The splicing/transitional period with my father was smooth, graceful, and slow, instead of the sudden shock for my father when Tim died in 1946. I'm satisfied to be doing what I really love and feel and that the pursuit is meaningful. I have not been conventional in my actions, nor have I followed any mold or patterns, but rather, pursued some ideas that, to some, seem unusual. But, always the actions have been built on solid, constant, and thorough training and tradition. And certainly the accomplishments have been successful, rewarding, and exciting for me.

During this period of branching out, I have been fortunate to be part of the heritage of Tim, my uncle, and Milton, my father. It is rewarding to feel their influence throughout the office. We have been in existence for more than seventy-five years (the oldest firm west of the Mississippi), and have served some clients for more than forty years.

There are different people now, though Bill Hutcheson and Lee Greenfield have been with the firm over 35 years. All of the members of the firm are inspirational individuals who share my enthusiasm to be innovative and creative. It is an increasing challenge to keep growth for growth's sake out of our list of goals as we continue to challenge large firms—but that too, is the challenge.

I couldn't be head of a big firm. I wouldn't have as much fun. Also, of course, I'd have to be too much of an administrator and become out of touch with our clients and the projects.

Our basic tenet—commitment to individuals, and person to person contact with the principals—can only occur in a medium-sized, very personal firm such as ours. Our way of working seems increasingly threatened by the corporate structure and their policies of expansion and departmentalization that ultimately results in the dilution of responsibility.

Growth and size imply stability and comfort, when in fact they simply provide a means by which responsibility can be avoided. With size and growth too often a client does not obtain and benefit from the personal input and creativity of the principals and key people. We continue to develop approaches which we hope will keep us unique and illustrate our belief that we can bring something special to a project.

The guiding force behind the firm is the total commitment to the understanding and recognition of what energy really means in all its ramifications. For instance, the world has produced all the energy needed for us now and for all the growth and expansion of the future world. As Bucky Fuller said years ago, simplicity, recycling, lightness, miniaturization are the keys.

We should not be in a "what are you going to do for me" society, but rather a part of "what can I contribute, and do for you?" community. The fact is, my greatest satisfactions come not from the creation of a new monument, but from the relationship with the people who are my clients and their happiness with what has been created to meet their needs.

Just as our profession lacks total commitment to living with nature and minimizing our use of resources, our profession also lacks a commitment to lasting quality. We are often guilty of responding to this year's or this decade's design fad. Though the ideas of integration of art with architecture, "ornamentation," and the use of classic principles are certainly valid alone, "Post Modernism" is not completely responsible, nor does it fulfill our mandate to contribute to living within our universe.

I feel somewhat like an explorer, searching and listening for clues regarding basics and simplicity, acting as a conduit, bringing light and energy sources into architecture. It is an exciting journey, very often slow, sometimes frustrating, but with no beginning and no end. Rather it is a constant voyage of discovery supported by the friendship and respect of the individuals who are my constant source.

February 1984

LIST OF PROJECTS: 1908-1983

YEAR	PROJECT	LOCATION
1908-1918	Stephens & Company Offices	San Francisco, California
	Herzstein Building	San Francisco
	McEwen Brothers Building	San Francisco
	Claus Spreckles Building Alterations	San Francisco
	Church, Our Lady of the Wayside	Portola Valley, California
	Kyle-Clementina Street Building	San Francisco
	Faxon Building (Hotel)	San Francisco
	Dr. Black Building	San Francisco
	Hotel Pennsylvania	San Francisco
1910-1951	Metropolitan Life Insurance Company Pacific Coast Headquarters	San Francisco
1919-1922	Jefferson School	San Francisco
	Brickell Residence	San Francisco
	Gunn Residence	San Francisco
	Naify Residence	San Francisco
	Paul Pflueger Residence	San Francisco
	Family Farm Camps #104, 31, etc.	Portola Valley
1922-1928	Castro Theater	San Francisco
	Alamo School	San Francisco
	Roosevelt Junior High School	San Francisco
	Theaters	Chico, Oroville, Tulare, California
	San Francisco Stock Exchange	San Francisco
	Alhambra Theater	San Francisco
1925	Pacific Telephone & Telegraph Company Headquarters Building	San Francisco
1929-1930	450 Sutter Medical Dental Building	San Francisco
	Pacific Coast Stock Exchange and Office Building	San Francisco
	Family Farm/Tavern, Outdoor Dining, etc.	Portola Valley
1931	Paramount Theater	Oakland, California
	Spencer Buckbee Residence Alterations	San Francisco
	Bethlehem Steel Company Building	San Francisco
1931-1951	George Washington High School	San Francisco
1933	Standard Oil Company of California Prototype Service Station	San Francisco
	Bal Tabarin Night Club	San Francisco
1934	Pacific Greyhound Corporation Shops	San Francisco
	Fairmont Hotel, Circus Lounge	San Francisco

1935-1936	Motion Picture Theaters El Rey; Royal; New Mission; New Fillmore; Coronet	San Francisco
1937	San Francisco-Oakland Bay Bridge	San Francisco
	Family City Club Alterations	San Francisco
	Pausons Store Alterations	San Francisco
1938	Florist Shop, Angelo J. Rossi	San Francisco
1939	Golden Gate International Exposition Federal Building California State Building California Auditorium Court of the Pacific	San Francisco
	Livingston Brothers Store Alterations	San Francisco
	St. Francis Hotel, Patent Leather Lounge	San Francisco
	Mark Hopkins Hotel, Top of the Mark	San Francisco
	I. Magnin Store Interiors	Los Angeles, California
1940	Abraham Lincoln High School	San Francisco
	Vollmer Residence	San Francisco
1941	Mark Hopkins Hotel, Broadcast Stations	San Francisco
	United States Army General Depot	Ogden, Utah
	Delprat Residence	San Francisco
1942	Science Building; Gymnasiums; Horticulture; and Athletic Field	City College of San Francisco
	Union Square Garage and Plaza	San Francisco
1945	Hunter's Point Theater	San Francisco
1946	I. Magnin & Company Store Building	Beverly Hills, California
	Department of State Transmitter Buildings	Dixon and Delano, California
	J.E. French Building	San Francisco
	Associated Broadcasting Studios	San Francisco
	Office of War Information, Radio Station	San Francisco
	U.S. War Housing	San Francisco, Vacaville, Fairfield and Albany, California
1947	I. Magnin & Company Store Building	Santa Barbara, California
	Paul Pflueger Residence	Hillsborough, California
1948	Master Plan	University of San Francisco
	I. Magnin & Company Store Building at Union Square	San Francisco
	Mt. Zion Hospital	San Francisco
	Ames Harris Neville Factory/Warehouse	Berkeley, California
1949	San Francisco Museum of Modern Art Alterations	San Francisco
	Civic Center—City Hall, Hall of Justice	Richmond, California
1950	H. Brandenstein Residence	San Francisco
	Crocker-Citizens National Bank	Oakland
	Civic Center—Public Library	Richmond
	Mills Hospital Additions and Alterations	San Mateo, California

1951	St. Ignatius High School Gymnasium	San Francisco
	Crocker-Citizens National Bank	San Francisco
	Civic Center—Auditorium/Arts Center	Richmond
	Gleeson Library	University of San Francisco
1952	Permanent Specialty Facilities	Fort Ord, California
	Telephone Exchange Building	Fort Ord
	Department of Highway Patrol	Sacramento, California
1953	Mills College Library Addition	Oakland
	Pacific Coast Stock Exchange Alterations	San Francisco
	Sumitomo Bank Alterations	San Francisco
	Darwin Bryan Residence	Fairfield
1954	Department of Motor Vehicles Headquarters Building	Sacramento
	Cloud Hall	City College of San Francisco
	Alta Bates Hospital Addition	Berkeley
	Golden Gate Bridge & Highway District Storage, Shops, Warehouse	San Francisco
1955	Phelan Hall	University of San Francisco
	Armstrong Cork Company Showroom/Offices	San Francisco
	Field Maintenance Plant	Fort Ord
	Crocker-Citizens National Bank	San Francisco
	St. Matthews Church	San Mateo
	Ebenezer Lutheran Church	San Francisco
	Smith Hall	City College of San Francisco
	Olympic Club Alterations	San Francisco
1956	Stanford University, Florence Moore Hall	Stanford, California
	Public Housing, San Francisco Housing Authority	San Francisco
	University of California, Medical Center Moffitt Hospital	San Francisco
	W.P. Fuller & Company, Laboratory Building	So. San Francisco
	I. Magnin & Company, Primavera Room	San Francisco
1957	Berkeley Civic Center (Study)	Berkeley
	Pacific Metals Company	San Francisco
	Dinkelspiel Memorial Auditorium	Stanford University
	St. Mary's College, Residence Building	Moraga, California
1957-1966	Crocker National Bank One Montgomery Headquarters Alterations	San Francisco
1958	St. Matthew Church Addition and Alterations	San Mateo
	National Park Service, Geochem Laboratory	Hilo, Hawaii
	University of California Medical Center Millberry Union	San Francisco
	Armstrong Cork Company Showroom Facilities	San Francisco
	City Hall; Civic Center Master Plan	Sunnyvale, California
	University of California Bevetron Addition & Bubble Chamber	Berkeley
	College of the Holy Names Academic Facilities; Gymnasium; Faculty and Student Residences; Chapel; Administration; Library	Oakland

1959	Xavier Hall Faculty Residence	University of San Francisco
	University of California Medical Center/ Millberry Combined Structure	San Francisco
	California Academy of Sciences, Library	San Francisco
	Memorial Gymnasium; Sutro Library; and Phelan Hall Addition	University of San Francisco
	St. Mary's College President's Residence	Moraga, California
1960	Strom Residence	Marin County, California
	St. Mary's College Student Residence	Moraga
	First National Bank of San Rafael	San Anselmo, California
	College of the Holy Names Student Residence Addition	Oakland
	City Hall	Modesto, California
	Union Square Garage, Alterations	San Francisco, California
1961	Flower Stand/Geary and Powell	San Francisco
	Gerow House	Marin County
	St. Mary's College Worker and Student Residences	Moraga
	Kendrick Hall, School of Law	University of San Francisco
	Lemoore Naval Air Station	Lemoore, California
	Civic Center Library	Sunnyvale
	Public Safety Building	El Cerrito, California
	Arts and Classroom Building	City College of San Francisco
1962	Mare Island Naval Station Missile School	Vallejo, California
	El Retiro—Loyola Hall	Los Altos, California
	St. Mary of the Palms Serra Center for Girls	Fremont, California
	University of California Medical Center Alteration	San Francisco
	University of California Cyclotron/Bevetron Buildings, Additions	Berkeley
	Crocker Bank Branch	Pebble Beach, California
1963	6th Floor Housing Additions	University of San Francisco
	Alta Bates Hospital Additions	Berkeley
	Crittinden House Alterations	Tiburon, California
	Lloyd David House Alterations	Ross, California
	Hotel and Restaurant School	City College of San Francisco
1964	Harney Science Center	University of San Francisco
	Pine Terrace Condominium Apartments	San Francisco
	Police Communications Building	Modesto
	SPCA Animal Shelter and Administration	San Francisco
	Water Department Corporation Yard	San Francisco
1965	Gillson Hall	University of San Francisco
	Crocker National Bank Branch	San Francisco
	Dental Clinic—Army Terminal	Oakland
	I. Magnin & Company Store Interiors	Oakland
	Lehr House	San Mateo
	College of the Holy Names Kennedy Arts Center	Oakland

	City Hall Competition—3rd Prize	Santa Rosa, California
	Law School Remodeling	Stanford University
	Clinical Sciences Addition	Stanford Hospital
1966	University Center	University of San Francisco
	College of the Holy Names Classroom Building Student Residence	Oakland
	Crocker Bank Service Center	San Francisco
	Medical School Computer Center	Stanford University
	Graduate School of Business	Stanford University
	Crocker National Bank Alterations	San Francisco
1967	Alterations to Campion Hall	University of San Francisco
	Washington University Law School Competition	St. Louis, Missouri
	Hayes-Healy Hall	University of San Francisco
	California Academy of Sciences Cowell Hall	San Francisco
	SPCA Animal Hospital	San Francisco
	Center for Biological Sciences	Stanford University
	Schwabacher & Company Alterations	San Francisco
	Shriners Hospital for Crippled Children	San Francisco
	Letterman General Hospital	San Francisco
	Oakland Naval Hospital	Oakland
1968	Herrin Laboratories; Student Services; Educational Services; and Food Research Institute	Stanford University
	Conlan Hall/Educational Services	City College of San Francisco
	Visual Arts Building	City College of San Francisco
	School of Nursing	University of San Francisco
	Crocker National Bank Branch 16th and Mission	San Francisco
	Crocker National Bank Data Center	San Francisco
	U.S. Navy Bachelor Officers Quarters	San Francisco
	Silas B. Hayes Army Hospital	Ford Ord, California
1969	Loyola Hall Alterations	University of San Francisco
	Smith Hall Addition; Creative Arts Addition; and Student Union	City College of San Francisco
1970	Computer Center; Theater and School of Education; Center for Behavioral Sciences; and Russell Room	University of San Francisco
	Lincoln University Program and Master Plan	San Francisco
	PG&E Headquarters Alterations	San Francisco
1971	Smith Hall Addition	City College of San Francisco
	Science Building Alterations	City College of San Francisco
1972	Rare Book Room	University of San Francisco
	Oakland Paramount Theater Restoration Consultation	Oakland
1973	Hermann Safe Company Offices	San Francisco
	SPCA Animal Shelter Additions	San Francisco
	Masonic Temple Additions (Study)	San Francisco

1974	Alamo School Remodeling	San Francisco
	California Academy of Sciences	San Francisco
	Animal Shelter	Hayward, California
	McLaren School of Business	University of San Francisco
1975	Alteration for the Handicapped	University of San Francisco
	Pier 39 Waterfront Development; Study	San Francisco
	College of the Holy Names Dormitory, Lounge, Cafeteria Remodeling	Oakland
	California Academy of Sciences Wattis Hall of Man; Meyer Fish Roundabout; and Peterson/McBean Entrance Gallery	San Francisco
	State Energy Office Building Competition Winner	Sacramento
1976	Delaware Center	San Mateo
	U.S. Public Health Service Hospital Alterations	San Francisco
	New Walter Reed General Hospital, Garage and Interim Facilities	Washington, D.C.
	California Academy of Sciences Docent Facilities	San Francisco
	Village Hospital	Guatemala
	Corte Madera Creek Flood Control Study	Ross, California
1977	University Center Alterations	University of San Francisco
	The Crossroads; Study	Gilroy, California
1978	Athletic Facilities Master Plan	Stanford University
	Sierra Arts Foundation/Sierra Center Performing Arts Center	Reno, Nevada
	U.S. Postal Service Term Contract	San Francisco
	Kendrick Hall School of Law Addition	University of San Francisco
1979	Athletic Facilities Master Plan	University of San Francisco
	James Lick Bathaus Renovation Pflueger Architects' Offices	San Francisco
	Cityview Hospital	Los Angeles
	Florence Moore Hall Addition	Stanford University
	Graduate School of Business 4th Floor Addition	Stanford University
	U.S. Army Dental Clinic Standard Plans	Washington, D.C.
	Corp of Engineers Integrated Office Complex	Nevada
	Batmale Hall	City College of San Francisco
	Medical Office Building	Reno, Nevada
1980	Lone Mountain Campus School of Education	University of San Francisco
	San Jose State University Library	San Jose
	College of the Holy Names Performing Arts Center	Oakland
	Bay Street Condominiums	San Francisco
	1380 Howard Street Building	San Francisco

1981	Library Addition	University of San Francisco
	Energy Manual—Bank of America/PG&E	San Francisco
	California Farm Bureau Federation Headquarters	Sacramento
	U.S. Public Health Services Hospital Alterations	San Francisco
	McKenna, Conner, & Cuneo Law Office	San Francisco
	Santa Rosa Ferryboat Rehabilitation	San Francisco
1982	Tennis Facility	Stanford University
	Hilltop Office Center	Richmond
	Ingleside Hospital Master Plan Alterations	Rosemeade, California
	SPCA Alterations	San Francisco
	Nevada National Bank Headquarters	Reno, Nevada
	Roundhill Professional Center	Fairfield, California
	240 Pacific Office Building	San Francisco
	Guidelines and Master Plan	Mare Island, Treasure Island, California
1983	Orchard Professional Office Building	Vacaville, California
	Stadium Improvements	Stanford University
	Environmental Safety Facility	Stanford University
	Shriners' Hospital for Crippled Children Spinal Cord Injury Unit	San Francisco
	Health and Recreation Center	University of San Francisco
	Sports Center	University of San Francisco
	U.S. Navy Brig	Treasure Island
	Centre Point Office Center	Fremont, California

LIST OF ILLUSTRATIONS

This List of Illustrations includes identification of the illustration or photograph, the location, the date of the project, the name of the photographer or renderer, and the page number where the photograph is found in the book. These illustrations are therefore not included in the index.

Illustration Number

74-82. LELAND STANFORD JUNIOR UNIVERSITY, Stanford, CA, 1891-1967 (courtesy of Stanford University, Joshua Freiwald, Phil Fein). pp. 62, 63, 64, 65, 66, 67

83-86. COLLEGE OF THE HOLY NAMES, Oakland, CA, 1956-1958 (Joshua Freiwald). pp. 69, 70, 71

87-92. THE CALIFORNIA ACADEMY OF SCIENCES, San Francisco, CA, 1967-1975 (Rob Super; Lloyd Ullberg, courtesy of the California Academy of Sciences; Joshua Freiwald). pp. 72, 73, 74, 75

93. WALTER REED GENERAL HOSPITAL, Washington, DC, 1977 (Peter Xiques). p. 76

94-95. LETTERMAN GENERAL HOSPITAL, San Francisco, CA, 1967 (Joshua Freiwald). p. 78

96. OAKLAND NAVAL HOSPITAL, Oakland, CA, 1967 (Joshua Freiwald). p. 79

97. SILAS B. HAYES HOSPITAL, FORT ORD, Monterey, CA, 1968 (Joshua Freiwald). p. 79

98-99. WALTER REED GENERAL HOSPITAL, Washington, DC, 1977 (Peter Xiques). p. 80

100. U.S. NAVAL AIR STATION, Lemoore, CA, 1961. p. 82

101-103. SHRINERS HOSPITAL FOR CRIPPLED CHILDREN, San Francisco, CA, 1967 (Joshua Freiwald). pp. 84, 85

104. PINE TERRACE APARTMENTS, San Francisco, CA 1964 (Joshua Freiwald). p. 86

105. CALIFORNIA DEPARTMENT OF MOTOR VEHICLES, Sacramento, CA, 1953 (Joshua Freiwald). p. 86

106-109. CROCKER NATIONAL BANK, San Francisco, CA, 1950-1968 (Gabriel Moulin, Joshua Freiwald). pp. 87, 88

110. THE DREAM, 1969 (Milton Pflueger). p. 91

111-113. SAN JOSE STATE UNIVERSITY LIBRARY, San Jose, CA, 1980 (Robert Van Noy). pp. 92, 93

114. BATMALE HALL, CITY COLLEGE OF SAN FRANCISCO, San Francisco, CA, 1979 (Robert Van Noy). p. 94

115-121. BATHAUS, PFLUEGER ARCHITECTS OFFICE, San Francisco, CA, 1980 (drawing: Pflueger Architects, photographs: Robert Van Noy). pp. 99, 100, 101

122-126. CALIFORNIA FARM BUREAU FEDERATION HEADQUARTERS, Sacramento, CA, 1981 (Robert Van Noy). pp. 102, 103

127. CONLAN HALL, CITY COLLEGE OF SAN FRANCISCO, San Francisco, CA 1968 (Joshua Freiwald). p. 104

128. BATMALE HALL, CITY COLLEGE OF SAN FRANCISCO, San Francisco, CA, 1979 (Robert Van Noy). p. 104

129-132. NEVADA NATIONAL BANK HEADQUARTERS, Reno, NV, 1982 (Robert Van Noy). p. 106

133-134. SIERRA ARTS FOUNDATION/NEVADA NATIONAL BANK HEADQUARTERS, Reno, NV, 1982 (rendering: David Brodsley). p. 107

COLOR PLATES: 135-171

135-139. PARAMOUNT THEATER, Oakland, CA, 1931 (Rob Super, Roger Minick). p. 111

140. RICHMOND CIVIC CENTER, Richmond, CA, 1949-1951 (Phil Fein). p. 112

141. COLLEGE OF THE HOLY NAMES, Oakland, CA, 1958 (Joshua Freiwald). p. 112

142. SAN FRANCISCO STOCK EXCHANGE, San Francisco, CA, 1930 (Charles H. Hays). p. 112

143. CIRQUE ROOM, FAIRMONT HOTEL, San Francisco, CA, 1983 (courtesy of the Fairmont Hotel). p. 112

144. UNIVERSITY OF SAN FRANCISCO, GLEESON LIBRARY, San Francisco, CA, 1951 (Joshua Freiwald). p. 112

145. GOLDEN GATE INTERNATIONAL EXPOSITION, San Francisco, CA, 1939 (Gabriel Moulin). p. 112

146. GRADUATE SCHOOL OF BUSINESS, STANFORD UNIVERSITY, Stanford, CA, 1966 (Joshua Freiwald). p. 113

147, 149. STANFORD TENNIS FACILITY, STANFORD UNIVERSITY, Stanford, CA, 1983 (Robert Van Noy). p. 113

148. CENTER FOR BIOLOGICAL SCIENCES, STANFORD UNIVERSITY, Stanford, CA, 1967 (Joshua Freiwald). p. 113

150. DINKELSPIEL MEMORIAL AUDITORIUM, STANFORD UNIVERSITY, Stanford, CA, 1957 (Joshua Freiwald). p. 113

151-152. CALIFORNIA ACADEMY OF SCIENCES, WATTIS HALL OF MAN, San Francisco, CA, 1973 (Rob Super, Peter Gerba). p. 114

153-154. CALIFORNIA ACADEMY OF SCIENCES, MEYER FISH ROUNDABOUT, STEINHART AQUARIUM, San Francisco, CA, 1973 (Rob Super). p. 114

155. SHRINERS HOSPITAL FOR CRIPPLED CHILDREN, San Francisco, CA, 1967 (Joshua Freiwald). p. 115

156. SILAS B. HAYES ARMY HOSPITAL, FORT ORD, Monterey, CA, 1968 (Joshua Freiwald). p. 115

157. LETTERMAN GENERAL HOSPITAL, PRESIDIO, San Francisco, CA, 1967 (Joshua Freiwald). p. 115

158. WALTER REED GENERAL HOSPITAL, Washington, DC, 1977 (Peter Xiques). p. 115

159. BATHAUS, PFLUEGER ARCHITECTS OFFICE, San Francisco, CA, 1980 (Robert Van Noy). p. 116

160. SAN JOSE STATE UNIVERSITY LIBRARY, San Jose, CA, 1980 (Robert Van Noy). p. 116

161. ORCHARD PROFESSIONAL OFFICE BUILDING, Vacaville, CA, 1983 (Robert Van Noy). p. 116

162-163. BATMALE HALL, CITY COLLEGE OF SAN FRANCISCO, San Francisco, CA, 1979 (Robert Van Noy). p. 116

164-165. CENTRE POINT PLAZA, Fremont, CA, 1983 (Robert Van Noy). p. 117

166-167. CALIFORNIA FARM BUREAU FEDERATION HEADQUARTERS, Sacramento, CA, 1981 (Robert Van Noy). p. 117

168-171. NEVADA NATIONAL BANK HEADQUARTERS, Reno, NV, 1982 (Robert Van Noy, Bob Sexton). p. 118

172-173. SIERRA ARTS FOUNDATION/NEVADA NATIONAL BANK HEADQUARTERS, Reno NV, 1982 (form derivations: John Pflueger; model: Don Bennett). pp. 121 and 122.

174. HEALTH AND RECREATION CENTER, UNIVERSITY OF SAN FRANCISCO, San Francisco, CA, 1983 p. 122

175. COGENERATION FACILITY, UNIVERSITY OF SAN FRANCISCO, San Francisco, CA, 1984 (model: Don Bennett). p. 122

176. STANFORD ENVIRONMENTAL SAFETY FACILITY, Stanford, CA, 1984. p. 123

177. STANFORD STADIUM IMPROVEMENTS, STANFORD UNIVERSITY, Stanford, CA, 1984 (Robert Van Noy). p. 123

178. STANFORD TENNIS FACILITY, STANFORD UNIVERSITY, Stanford, CA, 1983 (Robert Van Noy). p. 123

179-180. ORCHARD PROFESSIONAL BUILDING, Vacaville, CA, 1983 (Robert Van Noy). p. 126

181-182. TREASURE ISLAND, San Francisco, CA, 1983 p. 126

INDEX

A

B

C

D

E

F

G

H

I

J

K

L

M

N

P

R

S

T

U

W

Z